PUB

G000152474

Surrey

Rosemary Bryant

COUNTRYSIDE BOOKS

NEWBURY, BERKSHIRE

First published 1998
© Rosemary Bryant 1998
Revised and updated 1999, 2002, 2006

COUNTRYSIDE BOOKS
3 Catherine Road
Newbury, Berkshire

To view our complete range of books,
please visit us at
www.countrysidebooks.co.uk

ISBN 1 85306 533 1
EAN 978 1 85306 533 0

Designed by Graham Whiteman
Photographs by the author
Maps by Lionel Larcombe
Cover illustration by Colin Doggett

Produced through MRM Associates Ltd., Reading
Typeset by Techniset Typesetters, Newton-le-Willows
Printed by Woolnough Bookbinding Ltd., Irthlingborough

Contents

Introduction   6

Walk

1   Englefield Green: The Barley Mow
(3 or 4 miles)   8

2   Chobham Common:
The Four Horseshoes *(5 miles)*   13

3   Shepperton: Thames Court *(4 1/2 miles)*   18

4   Ockham: The Black Swan *(2, 5 or 5 1/2 miles)*   22

5   Pirbright: The Royal Oak *(3 1/2 or 4 1/2 miles)*   27

6   Farnham: The Nelson Arms *(5 miles)*   31

7   Elstead: The Mill at Elstead *(3 1/4 or 4 3/4 miles)*   36

8   Chiddingfold: The Winterton Arms *(5 miles)*   40

9   Shalford: The Parrot Inn *(5 miles)*   45

10   Hascombe: The White Horse
(5 1/4 or 2 1/2 miles)   50

11   Albury: The Drummond Arms
(4, 5 or 6 1/2 miles)   54

12   Forest Green: The Parrot Inn *(5 miles)*   59

13   Parkgate, near Newdigate:
The Surrey Oaks *(5 1/2 miles)*   63

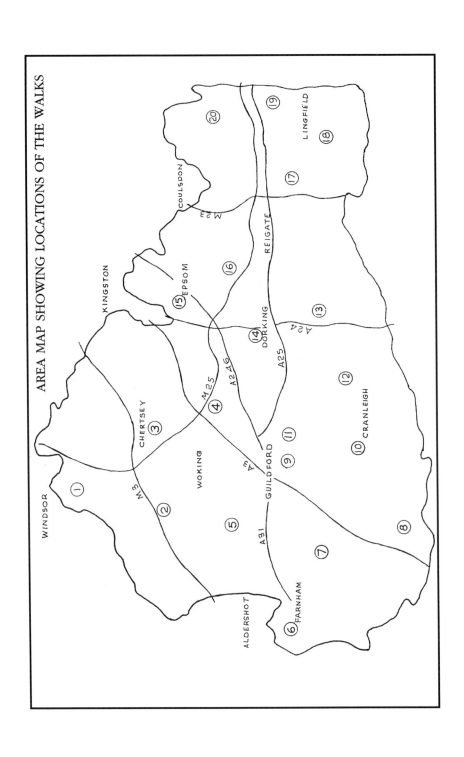

AREA MAP SHOWING LOCATIONS OF THE WALKS

Walk

14   Westhumble: The Stepping Stones *(4 miles)*   67

15   Stamford Green, Epsom:
The Cricketers *(3³/₄ miles)*   71

16   Mugswell, near Chipstead:
The Well House Inn *(4 miles)*   75

17   Outwood: The Dog & Duck *(5³/₄ miles)*   79

18   Newchapel, near Lingfield:
The Wiremill Inn *(4 miles)*   84

19   Staffhurst Wood, near Oxted:
The Royal Oak *(4 or 6 miles)*   88

20   Titsey Hill, near Woldingham:
Botley Hill Farmhouse *(4¹/₄ miles)*   93

PUBLISHER'S NOTE

We hope that you obtain considerable enjoyment from this book; great care has been taken in its preparation. However, changes of landlord and actual closures are sadly not uncommon. Likewise, although at the time of publication all routes followed public rights of way or well-established permitted paths, diversion orders can be made and permissions withdrawn.

We cannot of course be held responsible for such diversion orders and any inaccuracies in the text which result from these or any other changes to the routes nor any damage which might result from walkers trespassing on private property. We are anxious though that all details covering the walks and the pubs are kept up to date and would therefore welcome information from readers which would be relevant to future editions.

INTRODUCTION

Being always ready to enjoy good food at a welcoming pub; to explore Surrey's very varied countryside on foot, and happy to find fresh routes around familiar areas and perhaps some paths new to me, I was glad to be asked to prepare this book of pub walks in Surrey. I hope that you enjoy them as much as I have.

A wide range of pubs are included: some large, some small; some 'traditional', others in the modern 'family style'. They serve, as they have always done, as meeting places for relaxation, gossip and news or for rest and refreshment on a journey. Inns offering food and accommodation have provided for travellers through the ages, some becoming staging posts for coaches like the Barley Mow at Englefield Green. Others are former beer houses taking advantage of the trade associated with 18th century toll roads as seemingly in the case of the Winterton Arms, Chiddingfold, while later on 'road houses' sprang up to meet the needs of those 'out for a spin in the countryside' in a new age of 'motoring'.

Many are simply the traditional meeting place for a community when beer was the normal table drink for all ages and news came most often by word of mouth, whether it be local scandal or gossip, tales of a traveller or news from neighbours visiting a market or nearby town. G.M. Trevelyan, the historian, wrote 'in all ages the ale bench has been the social centre of the middling and lower classes of town, village and hamlet' although around the time of Elizabeth I the smaller gentry might also entertain their guests in a private room at the inn. Today clubs and societies still use pubs for their meetings but in the past many more gatherings were held, including Manorial Courts, parish meetings such as those of the overseers of the poor and, until the beginning of this century, coroners' inquests. Many of today's pubs have grown from simple cottage 'houses of sale' and the scanty history available and the nature of the buildings, suggest that this is how many in this book have developed. Licensing of these 'beer houses' in 1904 reduced the number and no doubt many that gained licenses increased their trade and extended as for example at the Four Horseshoes, Burrowhill or the Nelson Arms, Farnham.

A final group are those where an attractive or interesting building has been kept in repair by being put to a new use, as for example the Wiremill Inn, Newchapel, Elstead Mill and Botley Hill Farmhouse above Titsey Hill.

'I grant', said William Hazlitt, 'there is one subject on which it is pleasant to talk on a journey; and that is, what one shall have for supper when we get to our inn at night. The open air improves this sort of conversation or friendly altercation, by setting a keener edge on appetite.' All the pubs chosen not only provide a good starting point for a walk but make such conversations profitable. Simple food and good beer are available in all of them and many have a much fuller menu of well-prepared and imaginative dishes to be enjoyed in attractive and comfortable settings.

Please note that agreements for readers to use pub car parks while walking are on the understanding that you are a customer and that you will ask permission before setting off. If you are taking a picnic this must be eaten off pub premises. All walk directions start by assuming that you are *leaving* the pub, or at least have your back to it! The maps have been carefully drawn by fellow rambler Lionel Larcombe to show as much detail of the route as possible and the map numbers refer to the numbered paragraphs of the text. The relevant Ordnance Survey maps for each route are given: Landrangers at 1:50,000, and Explorer sheets at 1:25,000. These are a great help for checking or varying your route and using them alongside the sketch map and walk directions is an excellent way to become familiar with their use.

Throughout the preparation of this book any obstructions or maintenance problems encountered have been reported to, and dealt with, by the Highway Authority, from missing footboards on stiles to unclear paths needing additional waymarking. This is, however, a matter needing constant attention and difficulties can be reported, with as much detail as possible, including OS grid references or a street atlas reference with road names, to the Principal Rights of Way Officer at Surrey County Council, County Hall, Penrhyn Road, Kingston upon Thames, Surrey KT1 2DY or by telephone on 0845 6009009 – Highways Department; or email contact.centre@surreycc.gov.uk; or via the internet on www.surreycc.gov.uk. From time to time paths are legally diverted or restored to their definitive route, by the County Council as the Highway Authority. The altered route will be clearly signed and should cause you no difficulty.

It remains only to wish all readers the happiest of times in their explorations of our beautiful countryside and contentment in well earned rest and refreshment in one or another of Surrey's pubs.

Rosemary Bryant

① Englefield Green
The Barley Mow

The walk begins across the common to the Commonwealth Air Forces Memorial, with remarkable 360° views from the tower including the Thames, Windsor Castle and Heathrow Airport. Do include a visit to this tranquil place. The grounds are perfectly maintained, with spring bulbs and magnolias and a little later really attractive beds of dwarf rhododendrons. The walk continues through National Trust woodland and out across meadows at Runnymede to enjoy a stretch beside the Thames before visiting the Magna Carta and John F. Kennedy Memorials and returning via field paths to the pub.

The Barley Mow is a small weatherboarded building looking out over the green and cricket pitch towards the common. A very rural scene in an area described on a window in the nearby Commonwealth Air Forces Memorial as 'the heart of England, halfway between Royal Windsor and lordly London'. Tables out front make the pub look welcoming, and there's a roomy bar area leading through to a pleasant, enclosed garden with swings and a slide for children. George Eliot, the novelist, is said to have spent a night here when it was an inn used by stage coaches.

The pub is open from 11.30 am to 11 pm Monday to Saturday, 12 noon to 10.30 pm Sunday, and happily serves a cup of tea mid-afternoon. A choice of espresso or cappuccino coffee or hot chocolate is also available. The bar menu has steady favourites such as home-made steak and kidney pie, a selection of roasts, several fish dishes, ploughman's and baguettes, plus 'specials', while the puddings are tempting! Food is served from 12 noon to 2.30 pm and 6 pm to 8.45 pm Monday to Friday and 12 noon to 4 pm Sundays. There's Morland's Old Speckled Hen, Strongbow cider and Guinness, all on draught or a choice of Foster's and Kronenbourg lagers. Dogs are welcome outside at the front.

Telephone: 01784 431857.

- **HOW TO GET THERE:** From Windsor on the A308 to Old Windsor, then the A328 south for 1 mile. From Sunningdale on the A30 north for 3 miles, then the A328 for ½ mile. The pub is set on the edge of the green.

- **PARKING:** On the road alongside the green.

- **LENGTH OF THE WALK:** 4 miles, or 3 miles if you miss out the section over field paths at the end. Maps: OS Landranger 176 West London; Explorer 160 Windsor, Weybridge and Bracknell (GR 991713).

THE WALK

1. From the Barley Mow walk across the green, making for the top right corner, to a horse trough at the road junction. Cross over into Coopers Hill Lane. Walk up alongside the road or take a path on the left through the woodland going parallel with the road. This path finishes opposite an entrance to Brunel University Runnymede Campus, close to a road T-junction. Turn right, still along Coopers Hill Lane, to the Runnymede Memorial on the left which bears the names of 20,000 Air Force men and women who 'gave their lives for our freedom'. It is open from 9 am to 6 pm; weekends and public holidays 10 am to 6 pm. Detour through the gardens, if open, and from the far side of the cloister enjoy the view to the Thames below and beyond to the reservoirs near Heathrow airport and over the London basin. Slightly left (north-west) Windsor Castle stands out clearly. Even better views are gained from the top of the building over this remarkably well-wooded county. Pleasure boats

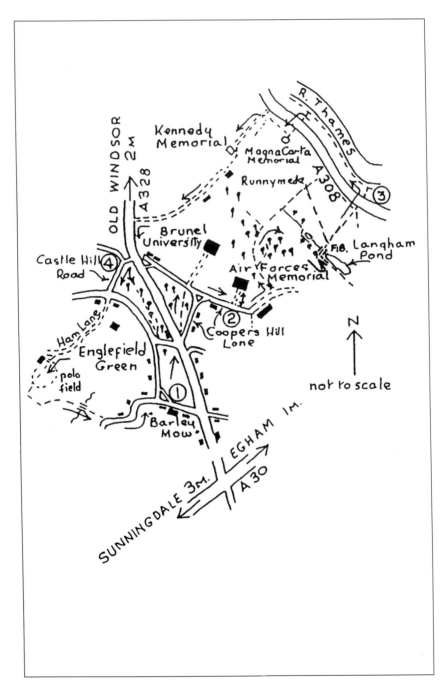

glide up and down on the river far below, aeroplanes fly low, and there is a great sense of detachment from the rest of the busy world outside.

2. Returning to the roadway, turn left to continue on, soon turning left and passing Kingswood Hall, part of the University of London's Royal Holloway College. Shortly after the road becomes gravelled, turn left through a kissing gate to go down Coopers Hill Slopes via steps. Keep forward past a path off right to the bottom. The National Trust now owns this 87 acre broadleaved, deciduous woodland, home to the noctule tree-dwelling bat, one of Britain's largest. The bluebells, yellow archangel and other woodland flowers are very pretty in spring, while I saw a jay and heard a variety of birdsong. Reach an information board at the bottom and pass a kissing gate left. Keep forward down the slope by a line of trees to a pair of kissing gates. Through the first kissing gate turn sharp right and enter the meadows of Runnymede, renowned as the birthplace of Magna Carta and also a Site of Special Scientific Interest. Keep along the bottom of the slope, with a fence and line of trees to your left, and reach Langham Pond. Upon reaching a clear area at the water's edge, turn back left over a stile to follow a board walk over the pond. Cross another stile, then head straight across these ancient alluvial meadows to a fingerpost and kissing gate by the road.

3. Cross over to the Thames, turning left along the bank on part of the Thames Path, a long distance walk of 180 miles from its source near Kemble in Gloucestershire out to the Thames Barrier at Woolwich. Continue for 1/2 mile past a little backwater, ignoring two fingerposts across the road, and on reaching a marker post (No. 7) with red and yellow bands, go left, crossing the road to walk ahead over the meads to the American Bar Association Memorial to Magna Carta where there are interesting information boards. On a summer's day you may well hear skylarks singing and see the Common Blue butterfly. Facing the Memorial turn right beside the hedgerow towards the John F. Kennedy Memorial. The path is on the left through a kissing gate and has 60,000 individually axe-hewn Portuguese granite setts and 50 steps, representing individual states in the USA. The overall theme is Bunyan's *Pilgrim's Progress* and a panel explains the design and symbolism. Beyond the stone Memorial to Freedom go left on an uphill path through bluebell woods, keeping ahead to a drive by a house left. Go forward up the drive beside the grounds of Brunel University left, through a gate, and follow it out to a road. Cross over and turn left up to a bus shelter near a road junction.

4. *For the shorter walk,* follow a footpath with yellow marker arrow at the corner of Castle Hill Road, through woodland to a road. Just before the road turn left on a horse ride between blue painted posts to emerge at a road junction. Cross over to walk across the green to the pub.

To continue the full route, turn right past a letterbox along Castle Hill Road and follow this beside woods on the left, to a crossroads. Go down Ham Lane opposite, past the imposing Castle Hill House, continuing as the track becomes unsurfaced between fields and goes through a gate with a kissing gate to one side. At a junction near a red brick house, go through a kissing gate on the left and turn right in line with a fingerpost. Keep ahead across a polo ground to reach a kissing gate by a track between two ancient oak trees. Through the kissing gate, turn left alongside the hedge to reach another gate. Go diagonally down the field to a kissing gate and footbridge over a stream. Continue uphill and head for a horse barrier to join a good path between gardens leading out to a road. Turn left along the road which bends right, left and right again before reaching the green and the pub.

② Chobham Common
The Four Horseshoes

The first half of the walk uses field paths and quiet lanes before returning over some of the highest parts of Chobham Common. The 1,500 acres is a National Nature Reserve, the largest in south-east England, reflecting the international importance of this lowland heath habitat. The view from Chickabiddy Hill includes the area where Queen Victoria reviewed 8,129 of her troops at the 'great camp' of 1853. Albury Bottom is wet heathland; the 'bee garden' here is thought to be evidence of the earliest inhabitants who cleared and first created this heathland.

The Four Horseshoes is set back across the green at Burrowhill, on the edge of Chobham Common. I'd often seen people relaxing outside on the porch or overflowing to the tables and it looked inviting! A quick glance at the map showed some new paths to explore so here was my chance. I now know why this old, low-beamed building, a row of former cottages, is popular with locals and passers by alike. It's cosy and comfortable with separate dining and drinking bars, a family room, a friendly welcome and good pub food. The cellar of the end cottage was once a mortuary so perhaps the local undertaker lived here. Means of earning a living in these parts for residents of yesteryear included turfcutting and grazing animals.

There is plenty of choice from the board, of starters, regular and special main dishes and desserts or simply a jacket potato or a ploughman's. I enjoyed a Sunday roast after my walk and other favourites on the menu include beef Bourguignon as well as vegetarian and fish choices. Food is served from 12 noon to 2.30 pm and 5.30 pm to 10 pm Monday to Saturday and 12 noon to 3.30 pm Sunday. On draught the beer is Brakspear's bitter, John Smith's, Jennings Cocker and a guest beer, or you may prefer Blackthorn's Cidermaster. Wine is available by the bottle or glass. Opening times are 11 am to 11 pm except Sundays when they are 12 noon to 10.30 pm.

Telephone: 01276 857581.

- **HOW TO GET THERE:** From Sunningdale south on the B383 for 3 1/2 miles or from Woking north on the A3046 for 3 miles to join the B383 at Chobham.
- **PARKING:** The pub has a large car park which you may use with prior permission, otherwise there is parking alongside the green.
- **LENGTH OF THE WALK:** 5 miles. Maps: OS Landrangers either 186 Aldershot and Guildford, 176 West London or 175 Reading and Windsor — the walk appears on the overlapping area of all of these; Explorer 160 Windsor, Weybridge and Bracknell (GR 970629).

THE WALK

1. Leaving the pub turn left along the road and soon left again along Steep Hill past a small pond. Just past the timbered Burrow Hill Farm, go left by a fingerpost through a tall side gate and down a drive. Go over a stile at the end and continue beside stables and between fields, turning right over another stile to a junction of paths by a small footbridge. Turn left between a field and garden to a road. Cross this and turn right for a few yards, ignoring the path through a kissing gate directly opposite. Go over a stile on the right of a driveway to Laris Farm, crossing the field diagonally to a small gate in the corner leading into woodland. Bear right through a second gate and continue, flanked by holly bushes, to a kissing gate and a drive.

2. Turn right to a small lane and then left along this, continuing beyond the houses to a farm track on the right with a fingerpost. Follow this past a row of poplars right and then, after it bears left, to a gate

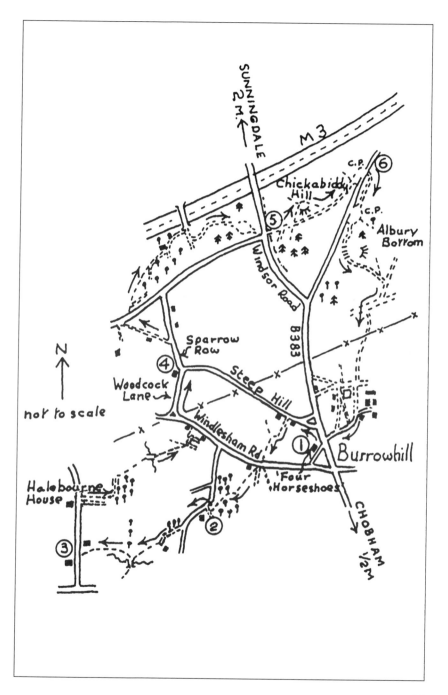

across the track near farm buildings. Go right over a stile to the right of the gate into a field. Cross diagonally to a stream running along the top of the field and keep this on your left, passing a hump-backed brick bridge and footpath signs left, but continuing along the right-hand bank, with further yellow arrows. Swing left with the stream and cross a double stile. Keep slightly right across two fields, via a stile to reach a gate and stile in the far corner. Bear left to keep alongside farm buildings on the right to a stile and gate ahead. Cross diagonally to a second stile and go across a small paddock to a stile leading out to a road.

3. Turn right, passing an Equestrian Centre. Just beyond a large house on the left, turn right by a gate along a fenced footpath with pleasant open views before entering woodland and swinging left to reach a footbridge and stile. Go diagonally right across the corner of the next field to a railed footbridge then diagonally left towards a fingerpost to cross another railed footbridge into a plant nursery. Keep left to join a concrete drive beside a stream. Continue beside the stream to the top corner of an open area, past a yellow marker post. Reach a railed footbridge and cross to the left-hand bank, following this out to a road. Turn left to a road junction, then right to walk up Woodcock Lane to a junction of lanes by the pretty timbered and thatched Fosters Farm. You may be surprised how many different wild flowers you can spot in the verges and hedgerows of these quiet lanes.

4. Keep ahead along Sparrow Row but soon fork left on a gravelled track alongside woods right. Pass a house left and continue on a woodland path to a road beside Pembroke House. Cross to another woodland footpath slightly right. The evening birdsong in the woods is delightful. Over a hundred species of bird have been recorded on the common! Keep left at a fork, always staying near the field edge, and finally, near the field corner, arrive at a junction where the path merges with bridleways. Here bear left, still with the field and bank to your left, to pass Oak Leaf Paddocks, then bear right, climbing through silver birches to a footbridge over the M3. Turn right here and almost immediately left, continuing parallel with the M3 but soon bearing right on gently rising ground away from the motorway. Continue over higher, more open, ground where the path at first keeps to the left and then bears right to reach a T-junction of roads.

5. Cross Windsor Road to a bridleway and go ahead beyond a vehicle barrier and crossing track, keeping over the common towards the highest ground. I saw several deer here and a fox during an

evening walk. On reaching a crossing path by a marker post detour left up to a small ridge, Chickabiddy Hill, to enjoy the sweeping views in all directions. This large tract of open heathland lies on the relatively infertile Bagshot Beds, a mix of fine sands and flint pebbles. To the north, across the M3, is the monument marking Queen Victoria's visit to review her troops. Turn right along the ridge and drop down to rejoin the main track. The gorse bushes in spring are a mass of vivid colour and smell strongly of coconut while later this area is purple with heather. Continue to a car park and road.

6. Cross the road and turn right along a horse ride parallel with the road to another car park overlooking Albury Bottom. An information board gives details of the insect, mammal and plantlife in this special habitat. Leave the far side of the car park along a broad path beside a seat, enjoying the amazing views eastwards. Follow the main path as it curls round the hillside, later descending a series of steps, and eventually, just beyond a signed footpath off left, reach a broad crossing track with marker posts, opposite a lone pine tree. Turn right to another broad crossing track with a marker post. Again turn right, going downhill, and shortly turn left, still following a blue arrow on the marker post, and go under power lines. Soon there are fields to the right. Ignore turnings either side, keeping forward past a four-way marker post, still with fields on the right. Reach a path junction with houses to the left and an electricity sub-station right. Still keep forward alongside the sub-station and join a drive, passing Gorse Cottage left, and follow this out to the road opposite the pub.

3 Shepperton
Thames Court

Riverside walks are always full of interest and this one starts at a busy and colourful area on the Thames near Shepperton Lock, then reaches a peaceful stretch through Chertsey Meads before crossing fields to follow the Wey Navigation to its junction with the Thames. Finally the foot ferry from Weybridge is used to return to the pub.

Thames Court has a long river frontage, making the attractive courtyard under a large Indian bean tree and the more open garden pleasant spots from which to watch the Thames traffic near Shepperton Lock. This large, comfortable pub with rooms leading off each other, some non-smoking and all providing cosy corners, is understandably popular with many family groups. Once it was simply a late 19th-century cottage, Weir Cottage, but the laying of a railway, piped water and electricity led to its enlargement and modernisation as the home of a succession of professional families until in the 1950s it became Thames Court, a guest house and private club where famous artists including Beryl Reid and Arthur Lowe appeared. Today there's still the sense of a large, happy house party.

Good food is served every day, that's 12 noon to 10 pm Monday to Saturday and 12 noon to 9.30 pm Sundays. The menu is a good choice of 'small' and 'large' plates and typical main courses include pies, steaks, hunters chicken with bacon and cheese, pork schnitzel, lamb moussaka or baked sea bass. On a winter's day at lunchtime the 3-bean spicy hotpot with crusty bread was a good choice. Freshly made sandwiches are available until 5 pm. The desserts are tempting and traditional and 'an extra spoon is free' states the board. Caramel apple grannie with custard, profiteroles, cheesecake and spotted dick are the temptations. On pumps are Bass, John Smith's and London Pride plus Carlsberg Export and Stella Artois lagers. Wine is served by the glass or bottle from a choice of six reds and six whites from around the world plus a rack of 'bin ends'. Opening times are 11 am to 11 pm on Monday to Saturday and 12 noon to 10.30 pm on Sunday. Children are welcome in the dining room. Well-behaved dogs are welcome in the garden.

Telephone: 01932 221957.

- **HOW TO GET THERE:** From Chertsey 1 mile east on the B375 then a right turn into Dockett Eddy Lane for 3/4 mile. From Shepperton leave the roundabout on the B375 at the end of the High Street, along Church Road. In 3/4 mile turn left down Ferry Lane and shortly after Shepperton Lock reach the pub.
- **PARKING:** In car parks either side of the pub. If in doubt about completing the circuit in time to catch the ferry (see walk details), start from the small waterside car park at point 5.
- **LENGTH OF THE WALK:** 4 1/2 miles. Maps: Landranger 176 West London; Explorer 160 Windsor, Weybridge and Bracknell (GR 071660).

THE WALK

Note: the foot ferry runs quarter-hourly on demand, starting at 9 am Monday to Saturday, 10 am on Sunday and finishing at 6 pm. For more details, call the ferry office telephone: 01932 254844.

1. Facing the river turn right along the bank, part of the 180 mile Thames Path from its source near Kemble in Gloucestershire to the Thames Barrier at Greenwich. Past the parking area for Pharoah's Island, reach a wide grassy area and continue along the waterside. Where the roadway leaves the riverside continue along the bank on a shady, grassy path. The houses thin out and Chertsey Meads are seen opposite. Notice an old Dutch barge with its mast and lee-board, and

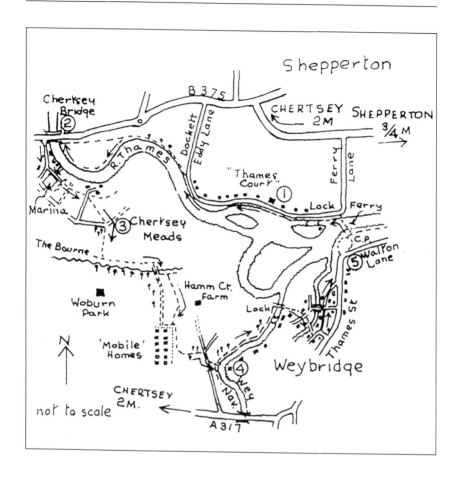

really permanent looking houseboats with well-kept gardens. At a kissing gate leading into the wide space of the water meadows, either follow the loop of the river bank or take a diagonal path to reach a kissing gate by Chertsey Bridge. Leaving the Thames Path, cross the bridge.

2. Turn immediately left at the end into Bridge Wharf, down a roadway signed as a footpath. Beyond the new apartment blocks, where a footpath goes off right by Bates Marine Sales, keep forward with bungalows on the left and a marina right to cross a footbridge. Reach an open area and head over the grass, crossing two broad tracks, towards the corner of gardens and a roadway. Across this ignore a well-walked route forking left and take a smaller one going diagonally right towards a line of large pylons. Reach a junction of lanes in the middle of this open grassy area, Chertsey Meads, one of suburbia's oases.

3. Cross to a clump of trees and keep ahead on a grassy path, No. 9, over the meadows towards a line of trees beyond power cables. Depending on when you walk, skylarks may be signifying 'the lazy, hazy, crazy days of summer' but take care, they nest among the grasses. At a crossing path alongside The Bourne turn left. Woburn Park is on the opposite bank. Staying beside the stream, reach a concrete bridge over the river tucked in a corner below crossing power lines. (There is a World War II pillbox, covered in brambles, to the left.) Across the bridge turn immediately left over a stile, following the river bank, shortly turning right by a fingerpost. Cross fields in line with the fingerpost and the central row of power cables, keeping a broken hedgerow on your right in the second field. Cross a stile and go slightly right alongside a line of trees and a ditch left, towards 'mobile homes'. Keep ahead over a stile alongside these on the right and open fields left. Cross another stile and keep forward for a short way to a fingerpost, at which turn sharply left across the field past a further post. Reach a stile leading through an area of scrubland to a lane by the entrance to Hamm Court Farm. Turn right and about 100 yards along on the left find a path which leads through trees onto the Wey Navigation towpath.

4. Turn left along a very quiet stretch of the Navigation flanked by woodland left and mature gardens on the far bank, and come to Thames Lock with a National Trust exhibition and information centre. Cross the footbridge and follow a concrete path signed to Thames Street. Follow the railings on the left, then cross straight over a drive to continue along the footpath opposite, crossing a footbridge over a backwater, to reach a small lane, Church Walk. Turn left and keep forward where this becomes a footpath, past a very pretty row of cottages. Cross a road and follow the path opposite, still Church Walk, finally emerging beside the Old Crown pub. Turn left along the road to a car park on the bend by the waterside.

5. Walk through the car park onto the towpath, the Thames Path, and a short way along, find the third set of stone steps, just past a seat, leading down to the ferry. Cross to Shepperton. Turn left along the bank, past Shepperton Lock with information panels on the Thames Path and the development of the river in this area, to the pub. Notice its sign, a perplexed drake with a frog squatting on its head.

④ Ockham
The Black Swan

A very varied walk through peaceful farmland with good views and crossing the disused Wisley Airfield. The full version goes over Ockham Common to visit Chatley Heath Semaphore Tower. There are demonstrations of signalling here, when open, and a rooftop viewing platform with telescopes giving stunning views all round between London and the North Downs. A 2 mile route, using field paths and woodland tracks near the pub, is also described.

The Black Swan, otherwise known as 'the Mucky Duck', sits alone at a country crossroads between Ockham and Cobham. While the sign at the front is of a black swan, don't miss the alternative one in the garden at the side: a white duck is being splashed with mud from a passing car! It's a roomy, well-used pub, popular with families and walkers at weekends and used as a lunchtime escape from offices on weekdays. A separate dining room has a verandah and tables outside and the garden provides views over the fields and a large play area for children with swings and a roundabout. On summer weekends there's often a barbecue and a bouncy castle. A field beside the car park is the home pitch for the pub football team and is also used for various dog training sessions.

Food is served 12.30 pm to 4.30 pm at weekends and 12 noon to 2.30 pm and 6.30 pm to 8.30 pm weekdays. At weekends there's a full menu but on weekdays it's bar snacks such as ploughman's or 'jackets' at lunchtime; and bar meals, for example a steak or lamb chops, in the evening. Sunday roasts are served from 12 noon to 5 pm with a choice of three roasts or fish with children's portions at half price — no wonder the dining room was crowded with family groups when I visited on a sunny Sunday. There were 5 regular real ales plus guest beers on my last visit. Ringwood's, Old Thumper, Porter 4X, Fuller's London Pride, Hogs Back Brewery TEA and Adnam's Broadside were the regulars and Sharp's Doombar and Welton's Pridenjoy the guest beers. Draught cider drinkers choose between Scrumpy Jack and Strongbow while wine bibbers may either have a glass or share a bottle. Well-behaved dogs are welcome. Opening times are 11 am to 11 pm on Monday to Saturday and 12 noon to 10.30 pm on Sunday. I got the feeling this pub, which is a free house, is content to be a 'happy-go-mucky' duck, leaving other places to aspire to the elegance of a black swan.

Telephone: 01932 862364.

- **HOW TO GET THERE:** From Guildford 4 miles north on the A3, then the B2215 through Ripley to the A3 underpass, then the B2039 for $1/2$ mile before turning left at the war memorial along Ockham Lane for $1\,1/4$ miles. From the M25 junction 10 take the slip road south for 600 yards, turning left onto a minor road (before the A3), signposted 'Effingham', for $1^1/4$ miles.
- **PARKING:** In the pub car park.
- **LENGTH OF THE WALK:** $5^1/2$ miles, or 5 miles if you omit the Semaphore Tower. A shorter circuit of 2 miles is also possible. Maps: OS Landranger 187 Dorking and Reigate; Explorer 145 Guildford and Farnham (GR 089573).

THE WALK

1. Cross the road to go a short way along Ockham Lane, towards Ockham, Ripley and Wisley. Turn left down a concrete farm road, signed 'Blackmoor Farm', just before cottages right. Continue down a dip and up the other side, and then some way between fields. Where the roadway branches right near a farm entrance, turn left onto a bridleway alongside an overgrown ditch. Enter a woodland and keep straight ahead, avoiding all side paths, on a path between banks. It is very pretty in May with bluebells everywhere. Keep forward, descending very gently and ignoring all side tracks, and finally swing left over a small brick-walled bridge and go up a slope to a road.

2. Go left and where the road bends sharply left, turn right down a lane, May's Green. Just before the lane divides turn left over a stile with a yellow marker and cross a garden to a gate and footbridge in the corner behind a garage. Continue between fences, then go over a stile and across a field to another stile and join a driveway between houses. Keep forward, going gently uphill with extensive views opening up to the right and behind you over the Mole Valley. Where the road swings left by Suma Farm Cat Hotel keep ahead on a narrow path to a kissing gate and steps leading down to a road.

3. Turn left, passing the distinctive pink painted Flower Cottage, to the top of the rise. Turn right along a broad track and reach a stile between gates on the left. An imposing house, Hatchford Park, is seen right while the Black Swan and its football field are across fields on your left.

For the shorter version from 3A, turn left over the stile and walk down the fields, crossing a series of stiles, to Old Lane. Turn left along the road to the pub, returning across the football field.

To continue the full route, keep along the broad track to pass large houses on the left. Keep ahead beside a barrier, following the bridleway onto Ockham Common. Avoid side paths and keep ahead for 400 yards to a clearing with a post and rail fence ahead and a crossing bridle track and fingerpost.

To continue without visiting the Semaphore Tower, turn left and go gently downhill on a bridleway signposted 'Old Lane'. Continue from point 4.

To visit the Chatley Heath Semaphore Tower, keep forward through a horse barrier and bear right uphill through birch and pine, following a sign of a sailor with a telescope. Bear right at a fork and follow further signs to the tower. This is open from late March to early October, 12 noon to 5 pm, on Saturdays, Sundays and bank holidays plus Wednesdays in Surrey schools' holidays and from the end of October to March 12 noon to 4 pm on the first Sunday of the month. There is a small admission charge. Telephone 01372 458822 for enquiries. The 60 foot tower was built in 1822, one in a chain of 15 former naval

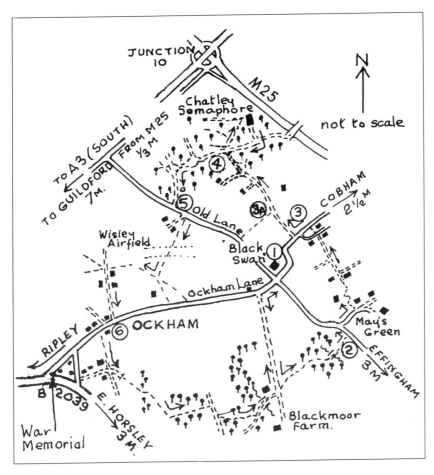

semaphore towers relaying messages between the Admiralty in London and Portsmouth Dockyard. Now managed by Surrey County Council, there is a small shop for souvenirs, maps and books, a Countryside Information Room and a picnic area. Note the well, only rediscovered in 1994 when overnight the ground subsided more than six feet!

Leave by walking past the picnic tables, with the tower on your left, and join a tarmac drive. Where this swings left, turn right to go steadily downhill on a bridleway bordered by rhododendrons, ignoring small side paths. Keep ahead through the open area which you crossed earlier, following the bridleway signed to Old Lane.

4. Continue downhill, following the bridleway as it swings right, and keep ahead across a more open area, ignoring a large track right and

other side paths, to reach a broad crossing track opposite a footpath with a barrier. Turn left along the broad track and, ignoring tracks either side, keep ahead past a field on the right to a gateway by a road.

5. Turn left along the road and shortly go right over a stile beside the drive to a house. Soon cross two more stiles either side of a drive, keeping along the field edge and then, at the corner, straight ahead. Suddenly you come to the runway of the disused Wisley Airfield. Cross this between barriers and keep straight ahead across cropped fields in a high, wide open area with extensive views in all directions over wooded countryside. An aircraft navigation beacon sits looking rather alien in this landscape! Over the next stile at the end of the field turn right, keeping along the field edge. Keep forward at the corner and reach a stile leading onto a farm track. Turn left along this, between farm buildings and past The Old Farm left and Bridge End Farm right, continuing as the lane becomes surfaced and goes downhill to a road beside Yew Tree Cottage.

6. Turn right through a pretty part of the scattered village of Ockham, passing Bridge End Cottage on the left. At the end of the garden wall, opposite Beech Cottage, turn left and immediately fork right to a field entrance. Cross a stile to the left of a field gate. Keep forward through woodland alongside a recreation ground, and cross a stile in the corner. The distinctive building seen to the right is the Hautboy Inn. Continue beside a hedge to a junction of tracks near a house. Turn left past the track continuing beside the house, to reach an open area with a fingerpost, by field entrances. Turn right here along a short track to cross a stile by a gate. Go diagonally left up a field to a gateway in the corner and through a belt of trees to the next field. Cross this diagonally right in line with a yellow marker and go over a stile into woodland with bluebells in the spring. I saw a white pheasant here. Reach a drive by the gate to Stumps Grove Farm. Turn right alongside a field and very shortly, at the corner of a wood, turn left beside a barrier along a woodland path. At a T-junction with a broader path turn left and go over a footbridge to join a concrete drive past a house on the left. Follow this drive as it turns left, with a gravel track off right. You have now rejoined the earlier route. Retrace your steps out to the road and turn right to reach the crossroads by the pub.

5 **Pirbright**
The Royal Oak

A fairly level, not too strenuous walk, mainly through woodland with stretches of open fields. If you have only driven by this area then here is a chance to explore. You will find Peat Moor which provided peat for local pottery kilns at the turn of the 17th and 18th centuries — and Henleypark Lake, a pretty spot, especially when the rhododendrons and waterlilies are flowering.

The Royal Oak is in the countryside a mile from the village. It's set back in a large well-maintained garden that is kept looking pretty throughout the year. The early blossom and daffodils are always eye-catching. I am sure you will be as delighted as I was when you go inside. The main bar area is much older than the exterior suggests, low ceilinged with a large fireplace, various cosy corners and a comfortable, contented air. A good fire burns when necessary. Food is served 12 noon to 9.30 pm on Sunday; 12 noon to 10 pm on Monday to Saturday. The menu plus a specials board provides a choice of interesting and carefully prepared food, for example lamb with honey

and fennel in a yogurt marinade, served with red cabbage. A speciality is a Pie of the Day and there are several vegetarian choices. Real ales are taken seriously here: this was CAMRA's Pub of the Year 2001 for the Surrey/Hants borders. Only traditional ales, local where possible, are served on hand pumps and there are regular 'ale festivals', Hogsback TEA, Morland's Old Speckled Hen, Greene King's IPA, Al Fresco and Abbot Ale was the choice on my last visit. The cider offered is Strongbow. Wines are also chosen carefully and an interesting list is well described: all are available by glass or bottle. Opening times are 11 am to 11 pm on Monday to Saturday and 12 noon to 10.30 pm on Sunday. Dogs are welcome on a lead in the garden. Children under 14 years are admitted to the garden only.
Telephone: 01483 232466.

- **HOW TO GET THERE:** The pub is one mile south of Pirbright on the Aldershot Road, the A324. From Aldershot 3 miles east on the A323, then 2 ½ miles on the A324. From Woking take the A324 through Pirbright to the pub. From Guildford 4 miles north on the A322, then the B380 west to the A324, turning left to the pub.
- **PARKING:** In the large pub car park but you must ask permission before leaving your car while you walk.
- **LENGTH OF THE WALK:** 4½ miles, or a shorter route of 3½ miles. Maps: OS Landranger 186 Aldershot and Guildford; Explorer 145 Guildford and Farnham (GR 944544).

THE WALK

1. Cross the road slightly left to a bridleway beside Stream Farm Boarding Kennels. Keep ahead through woodland for about 450 yards to a marker post on the right.

For the shorter walk, continue along the broad track, joining a driveway by the entrance to Bourne House. Keep forward to a road and turn right. Just before the entrance to an MOD area turn left beside a vehicle barrier, and follow directions from 3A.

2. *To continue the full route,* turn right towards a stile. Keep forward, crossing a small stream via a railed footbridge, on a narrow, winding woodland path, to a stile leading out across a field. Cross another stile ahead to re-enter woodland over a plank bridge. The bank on the left is a good stretch for bluebells. Where this bank turns left, take care to keep forward on a small twisting path through rhododendron bushes, passing a white metal gate right and soon an MOD Army Land sign left.

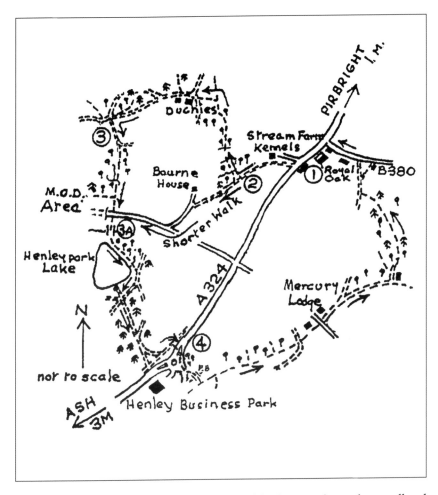

Turn left by a marker post opposite a paddock gate, through woodland of birch and pine, to a junction of tracks. Keep ahead towards a house, The Duchies. Continue along the track past the house, with fields left and paths into woodland right. Continue past Rail's Field and where several tracks come in from the right, by an MOD sign, turn left over a stile by a gate marked Rail's Farm. Near here is an old coaching route where in 1802 George III's coach overturned in the bog while he was on his way to Frimley. He had to put up at the inn in the village and his coach was stuck for several days.

3. Over the stile follow a grassy, fenced path between fields. Cross stiles beside a pair of gates, then keep straight ahead through

29

woodland, leaving the broad track which swings off left. To the right is Peat Moor. Just past a metal gate, reach a vehicle barrier and go through a kissing gate. Spot the camouflaged footpath sign! Cross the roadway ahead near the entrance to a military firing range, with views west across to Lookout Hill and Romping Downs.

3A. Go ahead over a stout footbridge. Bear left up the bank on a small path through rhododendrons, past a sign, 'Aldershot Garrison Angling Club', and a horse barrier, to skirt Henleypark Lake. Henley Park was a royal manor house until Charles I's time and the home of Lord Pirbright at the beginning of the last century where he was visited by Edward VII. It stood across the A324 from the lake, on the site of the present Business Park. Cross a bridge over the sluice, ignore a path immediately off right and come to a T-junction. Turn right and soon fork right again to reach a junction of five tracks. Bear left on gently rising ground out to a road, ignoring side paths. Near the road go left, parallel with the road, for about 100 yards to reach a marker post on the right. Cross the road by a roundabout at the entrance to Henley Business Park car park.

4. Follow the footway on the left of the entrance road but, when the roadway divides, leave it to keep ahead down the slope, to cross over a footbridge. Continue forward, with woodland left. At the top turn left by a yellow marker along a broad path. Ignore a smaller path off right and later turnings left, going through mixed woodland with views right to the Hog's Back. A green woodpecker flew across in front of me on this peaceful stretch. Keep forward across a drive and alongside a beech hedge to a kissing gate and a road. Cross to follow a driveway beside Mercury Lodge, going through a gateway marked Cobbett Hill Cottage and bearing right through woodland alongside a golf course. On reaching a house turn left in front of this by a marker arrow, keeping alongside the garden where the path forks. A small but distinct path winds through wet heathland, a diminishing habitat, and meets a broad track. Turn right, crossing a stream and bearing left out to a road. Turn left along the road and soon reach a road junction by Stanford Farm Cottage. The Royal Oak is a short way along on the left.

Farnham
The Nelson Arms

If you have not visited this historic market town before, do make this walk an opportunity to do so and delight in the many interesting buildings, the tiny lanes and the variety of shops. The well-signed Tourist Information Centre is in West Street. There are good views throughout the route which uses a series of quiet lanes and tracks over high ground above the town before returning along field paths. It's easy, pleasant going with very few stiles and you can enjoy the trees in Farnham Park on the last stretch.

The Nelson Arms is in the broad and elegant Castle Street, designed to hold fairs and markets and flanked by fine old Georgian fronted houses, which leads up to the Norman castle and keep of this historic and thriving town, overlooking the Wey Valley. The pub commemorates the town's connection with Lord Horatio Nelson, or more particularly his visits to Lady Emma Hamilton who lived across the river. It's a cosy old building with a low, beamed ceiling and in 1729 was already established as a pub, The-Hand-and-Pen. Nelson memorabilia is all around you, including what is claimed to be one of his glass eyes embedded in a post. What do you think? At least the landlord won't turn a blind eye and will make you welcome, as a multi-language sign outside announces. The hand-carved pub sign is also worth noting.

The English beers are from the local Hogsback Brewery, and the lagers are Fosters, Stella Artois and Kronenbourg. There is also Guinness and the cider is Scrumpy Jack. Wine is served by the glass or bottle. Food is served all day on Saturdays and Sundays but not between 3 pm and 6 pm on weekdays. In the restaurant there are some tempting starters and 90% of the 'specials' are homemade dishes. The choice ranges from liver and bacon with mash, to paella and other fish dishes, salads, steaks or a beef pie, plus vegetarian options. Children are welcome in the dining area. Opening times are 11 am to 11 pm on Monday to Saturday and 12 noon to 10.30 pm on Sunday. Telephone: 01252 716078.

- **HOW TO GET THERE:** From Aldershot 3 miles on the A324 or from Guildford 9 miles on the A31, to the Shepherd and Flock roundabout, then follow signs to 'Town Centre' for the Hart car park off West Street. The pub is in Castle Street.
- **PARKING:** The Hart pay and display long term car park. Free car parking in Castle Street on Sundays.
- **LENGTH OF THE WALK:** 5 miles from the car park. Maps: OS Landranger 186 Aldershot and Guildford; Explorer 145 Guildford and Farnham (GR 837470 — the Hart car park; GR 839471 — Nelson Arms, Castle Street).

THE WALK

1. Turn left from the Hart car park entrance, following a small roadway behind Waitrose and past the Hop Blossom, a Fuller's pub. Keep ahead out to Castle Street along a path, Long Garden Walk, past pretty, early Victorian cottages, emerging by an early 18th-century Georgian house with imposing wrought iron gates. Turn left and soon cross the road to the Nelson Arms.

2. From the pub continue up the street towards the castle and ascend shallow steps arranged in flights of seven, each with seven paces between. A blind 16th-century bishop was thus helped to go from castle to town, so you could test them out by shutting your eyes! Near the top go left signed to Farnham Park, going above the road on a bank.

You may wish to detour right to the Norman keep to enjoy views

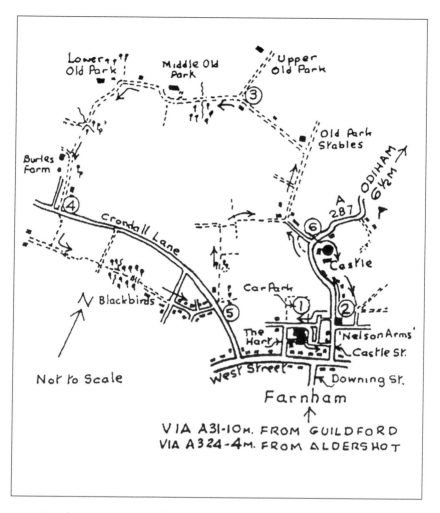

over Farnham stretching down to the river Wey. This is open between 12 noon and 5 pm on Fridays, Saturdays, Sundays and bank holidays, from 1st April to 30th September. There are also guided tours (modest charge) on Wednesdays between 2 pm and 4 pm of the Great Hall and other rooms. Enquiries: 01252 713393. To rejoin the path go down the drive by Wayneflete.

Where the path meets driveways into the castle grounds and before it continues by a railed fence, cross with great care to a footpath opposite, right of the drive to Bishop's Square. Reach a lane and turn left, passing a row of pretty cottages including The Cook House. Stay

33

on the lane, ignoring footpaths left, as houses give way to fields. Continue past a turning left and on reaching the next turning by Old Park Stables, go left along another old lane and past a farm left and then Brickfield Cottages right. I walked this early one morning when the lane was full of birdsong, the hedgerows full of dog daisies and a row of baby swallows were lined up on the telephone wires waiting for mother's return.

3. Where the lane turns right and continues uphill, by houses on the left, keep forward beside a gate to Middle Old Park. Go gently downhill to cross a stream then up through an avenue of oaks and past Middle Old Park on the right and a footpath off left, following a lane which now becomes surfaced. At the top of a rise, after passing Keepers Cottage right, there are good views left over Farnham to the hills beyond, while behind you a radio mast identifies Crooksbury Hill. Keep along the lane as it turns left and goes downhill passing Lower Old Park entrance before reaching brick parapets where a stream is crossed. As the lane swings off right uphill, keep forward through a kissing gate onto a footpath. Join a drive through a small gate and keep ahead, with a large house to the right following the drive to a road by the entrance to Burles Farm. Along this drive I saw baby bluetits feasting on the seed heads of cow parsley and heard a blackbird singing his heart out.

4. Cross straight over and go to the left up the bank by a fingerpost, curling round to cross a stile and walk straight up the field. At the top, by a fingerpost, meet a crossing track and turn left through meadows with open views over Farnham and towards Crooksbury Hill, gently descending beside a hedge left before turning left down steps to climb a stile. Turn right and keep forward alongside a bank right to another stile. Cross a lane and continue along a path opposite through woodland, crossing an open stretch before reaching a concrete footbridge over a stream. Go up steps ahead and continue out to a drive. Bear left along the drive to a road. Cross to an unmade road opposite, Wayneflete Lane, and follow this down to the main road.

5. Cross to a stile opposite and turn left onto a path beside a hedge left. Continue forward on this fenced path, at first climbing up and then through a dip with fields either side. At a fingerpost and a junction with a crossing path, turn right to walk down the other edge of the field with a hedge left and a fence right, with views over Farnham and ahead right to Crooksbury Hill again. At a field corner turn left and then right, ignoring a path left over a stile, to keep along the next field edge beside a hedge left to its end. The tower of Farnham parish church is clearly seen. Keep ahead to reach Old Park Lane opposite Grange Cottage. Turn right re-tracing part of the outward route but now follow the lane out to the main road.

6. Cross to the steps opposite and turn left on a raised path above the road. On reaching the corner of the cricket ground turn right by a finger post and gate and follow a path along the right-hand edge of the cricket field. There is a cafe on the far side of the cricket field by the car park, open daily from 10 am to 3.30 pm. At the end of this path, bear right to where an avenue of trees leads from the ruined castle on your right. Keep forward downhill and pick up a surfaced path leading to the right-hand corner. Go down a pathway between walls to a road, opposite a bowling green. Turn right along a lane leading out to Castle Street beside the Nelson Arms.

For an alternative route back to the car park from the pub, cross the road and turn right for a few yards. Turn left down an alleyway beside Keep House with a sign, 'to Lowndes Buildings', past a very pretty terrace of cottages. Continue between brick walls and at the end turn left down a small lane, part of Long Garden Walk. Partway down turn right along another alleyway between fences back into the car park.

⑦ Elstead
The Mill at Elstead

A gentle and varied country walk through fields, woodland and quiet lanes, the full route passing the very pretty and peaceful Cuttmill Pond.

Elstead Mill is most attractively set in 15 acres of its own grounds alongside the river Wey, on the edge of the village. An earlier building housed Cromwell's forces during the Civil War but the present one began as a large 18th-century corn mill boasting two sets of water wheels with their associated machinery and on entering you immediately see these giants. Built on four storeys, there is plenty of space, all smartly but comfortably furnished. Upstairs this Fullers owned pub and restaurant offers 'The Carvery Restaurant', overlooking the mill ponds. It is open Sundays only for roasts from 12 noon to 6 pm (8 pm in winter). Please note that this pub does not take bookings. On the ground floor is a series of separate rooms leading from the bar area while, in addition a small lakeside balcony, a large conservatory, a terrace alongside the mill race and plenty of seating on the grass beside the lake, all floodlit in the evenings, means you'll probably want to make a quick tour before deciding where to sit for the best view or to watch the busy ducks and admire the swans.

Bar food is served from 12 noon to 9.30 pm Monday to Saturday and between 12 noon and 9 pm Sunday. The menu features 'Small Plates' as varied as traditional Welsh rarebit and hoi sin spare ribs and 'Large Plates' such as steak and mushroom pie or seafood risotto, while I found the calves liver very good. 'Chefs Specials' are also featured and sandwiches are available. The draught bitters are Fullers house beer, London Pride and ESB. There's a blonde beer – Discovery – and the lagers are Carling Black Label and Stella Artois, Blackthorn cider and Guinness are also on tap. Wine is served by the glass or bottle. Opening times are 12 noon to 11 pm Monday to Saturday and Sundays 12 noon to 10.30 pm. No dogs allowed.

Telephone: 01252 703333.

- **HOW TO GET THERE:** From the A3 at Milford continue on the B3001 towards Farnham for 2 1/2 miles. The Mill is just beyond Elstead Bridge as you leave the village.
- **PARKING:** In the overspill car park but please ask permission before leaving your car while you walk.
- **LENGTH OF THE WALK:** 4³/₄ miles, or 3¹/₄ miles if you omit Cuttmill Pond. Maps: OS Landranger 186 Aldershot and Guildford; Explorer 145 Guildford and Farnham (GR 903438).

THE WALK

1. Walk out to the road and turn right. Just before the bridge turn left through a small gate onto a riverside path. The bridge is one of five in the neighbourhood dating from the 14th century and associated with the monks from Waverley Abbey. Cross a footbridge and stile and continue first along the water's edge then bear left between wire fences, crossing further footbridges. On reaching a stile just beyond where another path joins from the left, turn right out to a road. Turn right and follow the road round several bends. Soon after passing Fulbrook House turn right along a track signed to Broomfields Cottage and reach a small gate on the left by a fingerpost. Through this cross a field diagonally right to another small gate on the far side leading into woodland and follow a path through the woods to a road.

For the shorter walk, turn right, keeping along the road past Sugarbaker House to a road junction, and continue directions from 3A.

2. *To continue the full route,* turn left and just past a house, Cuttmill

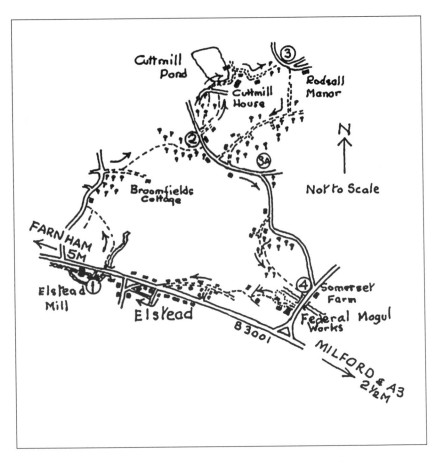

Platts, and the drive to Cuttmill Cottage, turn right by a fingerpost on a bridleway initially following overhead lines into woodland. Turn left on reaching a broad driveway and shortly, where the drive swings left, turn right to go over a railed footbridge to Cuttmill Pond. Keep forward on a path which curves round the pond, above Cuttmill House, to reach a drive. Turn right along this past Garden Cottage and an intriguing gateway to Willow Cottage, keeping forward on a path going steadily uphill through woodland and becoming quite sunken. Reach a small roadway and turn right, pausing for the view over a gateway to your right, across the commons at Elstead and Thursley towards Hindhead. The large house ahead is Rodsall Manor.

3. As the drive divides keep on the lower level, turning right down a stony track, an interesting mixture of ironstone and flints. Keep ahead, ignoring any side paths, through attractive mixed woodland where the track becomes very sandy and runs between old mossy banks. At a T-junction turn right, still on a sandy track but now going gently downhill. As you come to fields ignore all paths off left and stay on the track past a house, Broad Firs, and Kingshott Cottage with its pretty garden, to reach a road. Turn left, passing Sugarbaker House.

3A. At a road junction turn right towards Elstead down Attleford Lane. Just past Horseshoe Cottage turn right into a drive signed 'Molly Mackerels', and go through a side gate. Follow the drive past a house on the left and keep straight ahead between farm buildings and onto a grassy track which soon leads into woodland. The path winds down through the woods to cross a footbridge. Continue along the top edge with fields to the left and passing a Second World War pillbox. Cross a stile and head over a field beside the river Wey to cross a stile by the bridge onto a road.

4. Cross the bridge and shortly turn right into the car park of the Federal Mogul Company. Keep along the left-hand edge to a path between a fence left and a pumping station right. Continue past the works buildings and then go diagonally left across an open field used for clay pigeon shooting, to the far corner. Here spot a marker post to the right and follow the path to the right of a metal gate, which goes over a plank bridge and runs between wire fences before entering woodland over another plank bridge. Stay with this path as it twists through a strip of woodland then goes along its edge with woodland right and fields left to a T-junction. Turn right along a drive which later becomes surfaced, passing Elstead recreation ground and houses. Keep forward along Ham Lane, passing Broomfield off left, to reach the main road. Cross over into the road opposite, Springfield. Almost immediately turn right down Back Lane and come to a pub, the Woolpack. Keep forward across the green towards a garage and follow the road down to cross the bridge and reach the drive to Elstead Mill on the left.

8 Chiddingfold
The Winterton Arms

A rural walk through woods and fields with good views, visiting Dunsfold parish church, described by William Morris as 'the most beautiful country church in all England.'

The Winterton Arms is on the edge of this really picturesque village near the Sussex border. The rolling, wooded countryside is very peaceful and yet another example of the varied walking in this small county. Little is known of the pub's history. The present name recalls the Earls of Winterton from nearby Shillinglee but an earlier name was The Toll House. Until the 18th century the highroad through Hambledon between London and Chichester was 'notoriously one of the very worst roads in England' so a new route over Wormley Hill was doubtless thought worth the charge. It's a very sunny pub with an attractive garden and the comfortable bar, now 'saloon' and 'public' combined, has a friendly atmosphere and is well-used by local people and popular with walkers. A games room has pool, darts and TV. You can eat in the bar, the garden or a separate dining area. Children are welcome in the dining area and the garden where there is a fenced play area with swings, a slide and a bouncy clown while on hot days lollies and ice-creams are sold through the kitchen window.

Food is served on Monday to Saturday from 12 noon to 2.30 pm and 7 pm to 10 pm and on Sunday from 12.30 pm to 2.30 pm and 7 pm to 9 pm and is all freshly cooked. The menu, on a large board, changes daily. Wide choices are offered: eight types of ploughman's with generous portions, including Innkeeper's with a strong Cheddar; sixteen sandwich fillings, for example toasted bacon and Brie; five salads; ten alternatives for 'jackets' and a big range of snacks and main courses plus starters and desserts. So, with a children's menu too, there's surely something to suit everyone! There are always four draught ales, including guest beers and also four draught lagers, including Carlsberg, and a draught cider, Dry Blackthorn. Several house wines are sold by the glass, large or small. Opening times are Monday to Friday from 11.30 am to 3 pm and 5.30 pm to 11 pm, Saturday from 11.30 am to 11 pm, Sunday from 12 noon to 10.30 pm but the pub may close from 4 pm to 7 pm in the winter months.

Telephone: 01428 683221.

- **HOW TO GET THERE:** From the A3 at Milford go 4 miles south on the A283. The pub is on your left as you enter Chiddingfold from this direction.
- **PARKING:** There is a large car park at the rear of the pub. Please ask before leaving your car while you walk.
- **LENGTH OF THE WALK:** 5 miles. Maps: OS Landranger 186 Aldershot and Guildford; Explorer 133 Haslemere and Petersfield (GR 965365).

THE WALK

1. From the pub turn left along the road past Skinners Lane and attractive old cottages to turn left beside a drive to Lincolns Hill Cottage. Cross a stile and continue up the left-hand side of a field to a stile at the top. Head across the next field with views towards Hindhead opening up right. Go through a line of trees and turn immediately left in the next field, going gently uphill as Blackdown also comes into view on your right with its distinctive long, flat top and steep scarp slope. Just past a solitary oak and at the

41

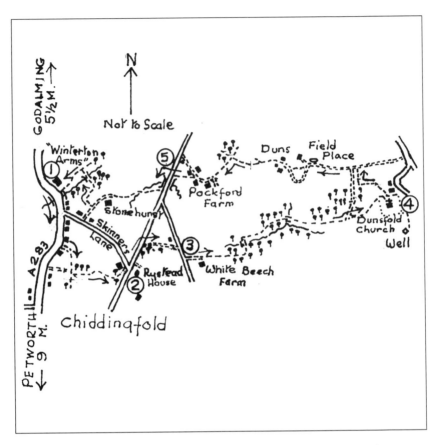

end of this field, go through a break in the hedge with a marker post, to continue in the same direction but now with the hedge on your right and descending gently. There are still splendid views and in turn from the left, St Dominic's School above Hambledon, Hydon's Ball and Holloways Heath are seen while beyond are the Surrey Hills. Pass a house left and enter woodland, almost immediately turning left by a marker post out to a road.

2. Turn right to a road junction opposite Rystead House. Turn left towards Pockford and Hambledon where the over-arching oaks, ash and chestnut make a lovely leafy walk. Just after the seventh telegraph pole, about 350 yards, turn right through a metal gate beside the road. Follow a broad track which diverges from the road, bears round to the right between old banks and reaches another lane beside White Beech Cottage. The double gateway opposite provides a view towards

Hascombe, lying in the gap between Hascombe Fort right and Holloways Heath left. Turn right along the lane a short way and go left by a fingerpost beside the drive to White Beech Farm.

3. Follow a fenced path past a large old barn conversion right and reach a lovely stretch through woods with badger setts. The path gently descends and curls left round the bottom of a field to cross a stream on a concrete bridge. Turn right alongside the stream with a field on the left, to a small gate, and continue beside the stream through woodland. This stretch has many wild flowers, including the pyramidal orchid and masses of wild garlic. Cross a stout timber footbridge and go through a gate into a field. Cross diagonally right towards a marker post on the far side and keep forward along the top edge of the field, with a hedge on your left. On reaching an opening in the hedge and a track up into woodland, turn left and immediately right through a small gate onto a footpath along the edge of woodland. A small metal gate leads into a field. Keep along the right-hand side of this to the corner. Go through a gate and keep forward beside the hedge on the right to a fingerpost beside the churchyard. Continue ahead through the gate and the farmyard to find the lych-gate to the church on your right.

This 13th-century parish church is $\frac{1}{2}$ mile from the village of Dunsfold, on a mound above the flood level of a river Arun tributary. The yew tree near the door is thought to be even older than the church. To visit the Holy Well turn right through the lychgate and go about 100 yards down a track. The water is said to be similar to that of Lourdes, rich in chloride and famed for healing eye diseases.

4. Leaving the churchyard either through the lychgate, built in 1901 as a memorial to Queen Victoria, or the smaller gate, but both with yew archways, go left up the edge of a small green. Turn left into a farm entrance. Pass the barns then go diagonally right across a field to a stile in the corner. Keep along the left-hand edge of the next field, turning right at the far corner to continue following the field boundary up to a stile and out to a farm driveway. Turn left. Where the drive divides near the entrance to Field Place, bear left towards Duns and soon go right over a stile. Walk down the field to another stile and rejoin the drive. Turn right to cross a stream and go uphill. Keep ahead through the gate to Dunsley Farm and at the end of the drive, past the house, walk over the grass going slightly right to a path leading through a gate and out along the right-hand edge of a field. Follow the field edge and ignore an opening by a gate right and keep on to the corner. Go forward over a small plank bridge and across another field. Turn left along the edge of a wood to a gate at the field corner. Join a track and keep ahead towards farm buildings. Cross the yard, past the drive going out right, and go through a gate in the far right-hand corner into a field. Go across this diagonally right to a stile on the far side and out to a road.

5. Turn left over a bridge and immediately right along a footpath. Cross stiles either side of a farm track, then a further stile and, keeping a small stream on your left, continue through a long, narrow field. Cross a stile by a gate at the far end to a junction of farm tracks. Take the one ahead going up the slope, passing a pond and farm buildings. Keep forward along the drive past the farm entrance, Stonehurst. At the end of the paddocks on the right, turn right down beside woodland on a bridleway which turns right and then left to go straight downhill to a footbridge over a tributary of the river Arun. Turn left beside the stream, then follow a fenced path across a field and finally through the yard of English Woodlands Ltd, to emerge beside the Winterton Arms.

9 Shalford
The Parrot Inn

A very varied walk with a pretty stretch by the Wey Navigation before returning over higher ground with outstanding views, especially north towards St Martha's church and along the line of the North Downs. It is enjoyable any time of year, with the best views when the trees are bare. Partway round, a canalside teashop at Farncombe Boat House is an interesting spot to tarry.

The pretty village of Shalford is dispersed around a very large green and common land just south of Guildford where the A248 crosses the Horsham road (A281). The pub has benches outside overlooking the common and a very attractive walled garden as well as a comfortable interior with a separated dining area. The proximity of Stonebridge Wharf, on the Wey Navigation, no doubt explains the presence of an inn for the past 100 years or more. Coal was brought by barge to the former Vulcanised Fibre Works where fuel tanks for Spitfire planes were produced during the war, while around the turn of the last century there was a brewery adjacent to the pub, and later a laundry.

Now all this has been replaced by the smart buildings of Broadford Business Park but you can still see the old gunpowder store, raised on staddle stones, a reminder of when gunpowder from the mills at Chilworth was taken from here by barge to London. Today the Navigation is owned by the National Trust and the wharf provides residential moorings.

I can endorse the pub's own declaration: 'A place for our guests to come and relax and enjoy good food, good wine, a friendly atmosphere and smiling faces'. The food is freshly prepared on the premises and served every day: Monday to Friday 12 noon to 2.30 pm and 6 pm to 9.30 pm; Saturday 12 noon to 3 pm and 6 pm to 9.30 pm and Sunday 12 noon to 3.30 pm. I enjoyed carefully cooked calves' liver and bacon. Choices include pork steak in an apple and calvados sauce, fish or pasta dishes, various pies including harvest pie as a vegetarian choice, or jacket potatoes. Sandwiches are something of a speciality from traditionals such as Cheddar and pickle to the exotic such as coronation chicken or bacon, brie and avocado, all listed on a separate board. It's a freehouse and the cask conditioned real ales are Fullers London Pride, Young's Special and Hogsback local brew — Parrot. The keg beers are Guinness and John Smith's and it is Scrumpy Jack for cider drinkers, and Foster's, Budweiser and Kronenbourg lagers also on pumps. The wine list has 'house selections' served by the bottle or glass. Well behaved children are welcome until 8 pm and dogs can join you outside on the green. Bed and breakfast accommodation is also available.

Telephone: 01483 561400.

- **HOW TO GET THERE:** From Guildford 2 miles south on the A281, then right onto the A248 to the pub. From Dorking 7 miles west on the A25, then the A248 for 4 miles, crossing the staggered junction over the A281 at Shalford.
- **PARKING:** In the roadway alongside the common, next to the pub.
- **LENGTH OF THE WALK:** 5 miles. Maps: OS Landranger 186 Aldershot and Guildford; Explorer 145 Guildford and Farnham (GR 998468).

THE WALK

1. Cross the road from the pub and turn left. Just around the bend cross Broadford Bridge over the river Wey then re-cross the road to follow the right-hand river bank on the towpath. This is peaceful countryside

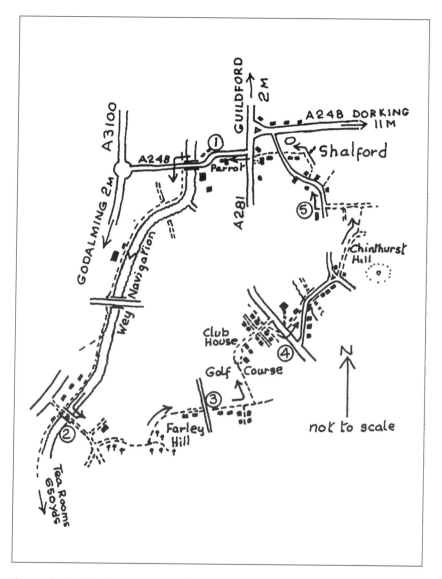

through Shalford water meadows, passing the junction of the Wey
Navigation and the Wey and Arun Canal and later the dismantled rail
crossing of the former Guildford to Horsham line, where a new bridge
is planned to complete a walk and cycle track. Note the World War II
pillboxes at intervals. Pass Unsted Lock and continue following the
towpath beyond a road bridge towards Farncombe. Farley Hill is seen

to the left. Soon after passing the garden of the Manor Inn reach a bridge by an attractive black and white timbered cottage.

(A short detour continuing along the towpath will bring you to Farncombe Boat House. Hector's on the Wey tea rooms are open 10 am to 5 pm, 7 days a week in July and August, and Wednesday to Sunday from September to June. Telephone: 01483 418769.)

2. Turn left across the bridge and follow a broad track between fields. Just beyond a bridleway left leading down past a house the ground rises to a junction of tracks. Here turn left on a bridleway which wends gently uphill beside woods with a lovely sweeping view down the valley and across to the Hog's Back. At the next junction turn left, crossing the head of this little valley and climbing more steeply now between high, sandy banks. A pretty spot in the spring for bluebells, violets and wild garlic and in the autumn for sweet chestnuts. Notice the lumps of ironstone in the sand. As you gain the top you are rewarded with an extensive view left along the line of the Hogs Back, the tail end of the North Downs; through the Wey gap in which Guildford sits with Woking in the distance; and right Pewley Downs and the Chantries with St Martha's church on the hilltop. Wonderful! Beyond Foxburrow Cottage the track becomes a small lane and shortly reaches a road.

3. Go through a gate opposite, keeping along the boundary of Bramley Golf Course. As the path becomes enclosed between hedges and banks, ignore a path off right and soon views open up across the fields on the right to the hills around Hascombe and Thorncombe Street. Just as the path begins to descend turn left through a kissing gate. Keep straight ahead across the golf course in line with a marker arrow, past fir trees and birches, and follow further marker posts, turning down the slope towards the club buildings. Continue past these to the end of the car park. Bear right and follow the drive down towards the main road. However, just before reaching this turn right by a marker post on a footpath which goes diagonally to the road opposite the entrance to Gosden House School.

4. Cross the road to the green at Gosden Common. The first women's cricket match was played on this common on 26th June 1745 between 'eleven maids of Bramley and eleven maids of Hambledon', states a plaque on the pavilion. Walk the length of the green past the cricket pavilion and join the road at the corner. The first bridge crosses a branch of the Wey and the second a defunct railway line and the bed of the old Wey and Arun Canal, now the Wey South Path. Over the bridge, by detouring round to the right, you can see a second bridge built for

the barge horses where the towpath crossed from one side to the other. Continue up the road to a T-junction and keep ahead up a track, part of the Downs Link, a 32 mile bridleway route linking the North and South Downs national trails. You are gently climbing with Chinthurst Hill on your right and once again good open views. Behind you to the left are the spires of Charterhouse School above Godalming. Reach a stile ahead where the bridleway turns off right, with a splendid view across to St Martha's church. To the left is Guildford Cathedral tower on Stag Hill. Cross the stile and follow the fenced path down to another stile and gate. Turn left along a green lane between hedges to a stile leading into a road on the outskirts of Shalford.

5. Turn right. Ignore the first footpath right by Field Gate House and continue to another beyond the letterbox and just past Greenhill. A fingerpost is half hidden in the trees. Turn right on this path which soon turns left past gardens to emerge at the corner of Shalford green with a pond across to the right. Go down the left-hand side of the green towards a wooden pavilion. Cross the road (the A281) near the junction with Broadford Road (the A248) opposite and walk beside this across Shalford Common to the Parrot.

⑩ Hascombe
The White Horse

This is a varied walk with pleasant views throughout. It starts through woodland, climbing over the greensand ridge, before descending to field paths and a quiet lane, with the return route passing close to the site of an Iron Age hill fort. The Victorian parish church of St Peter, rebuilt by Woodyer, is of local stone and has fascinating wall paintings of St Peter and other disciples catching fish.

The White Horse, which once had a sign painted by Gertrude Jekyll, is tucked away in the south west corner of the county, among the greensand hills, and has been deservedly popular for many years both for its welcome and excellent food. There are cosy saloon bar areas, a public bar and plenty of seats among the fruit trees in the garden. It has served as an inn at a junction of roads and tracks in this small hamlet, for several centuries. Built of the local bargate stone, it dates from the 16th and 17th centuries and it is thought to have been provided by the Lords of the Manor in whose ownership the inn remained until 1819. In 1863, while the church was rebuilt, services were held in a room here.

Photographs in the pub date from the early part of the last century when it was owned by Lascalles Tickner, a Guildford brewer.

Food is served on weekdays from 12 noon to 2.30 pm and from 7 pm to 10 pm, and Saturdays and Sundays from 12 noon to 2.30 pm. Choices from the menu include several fresh fish dishes, and a wide choice of mains such as pan-fried veal schnitzel, venison steak with red wine and cranberry jus, plus a traditional roast on Sundays. There's also a choice of salad-filled sandwiches or baguettes. The desserts are a big temptation but don't disappoint those who yield. You could try chocolate and hazelnut brownie, but then what about lemon and lime tart? There are 'Kids Meals' but children are not allowed in the public bar. The draught beers are Adnam's Bitter, Harvey's Best Sussex Bitter or Guinness and the lagers Stella Artois, Carlsberg or Grolsch Premium. The cider is Strongbow. Opening times are Monday to Friday 11 am to 3 pm and 5.30 pm to 11pm, Saturday all day, 11 am to 11 pm and Sunday from 12 noon to 10.30 pm.

Telephone: 01483 208258.

- **HOW TO GET THERE:** From Godalming 3 miles south on the B2130.
- **PARKING:** In the pub car park with permission or opposite on the verge
- **LENGTH OF THE WALK:** The full walk is 5^1/$_4$ miles but a shorter version, which is 2^1/$_2$ miles, is also possible. Maps: OS Landranger 186 Aldershot and Guildford; OS Explorer 145 Guildford and Farnham and 134 Crawley and Horsham (GR 001394).

THE WALK

1. With the pub behind you, turn right along Church Road and walk past the church and old cottages, circling the pond to where the pavement ends and the lane swings sharply left below School House. Here keep forward up the hill onto a bridleway, beside the entrance to School House. Continue uphill on this well-used old track through woodland for 700 yards. Ignore a footpath off right and reach a junction of tracks, with a fingerpost indicating the bridleway continuing uphill and another off to the left. Go left for just a few yards then turn sharp right to cross a stile onto a footpath. There are splendid views here down the slopes in both directions. Continue along the edge of woodland with a field on your left, and go steadily downhill. Finally reach another stile and just beyond this turn down left and descend steep wooden steps into a sunken lane and bridleway.

For the shorter version, turn right here and follow the track for about

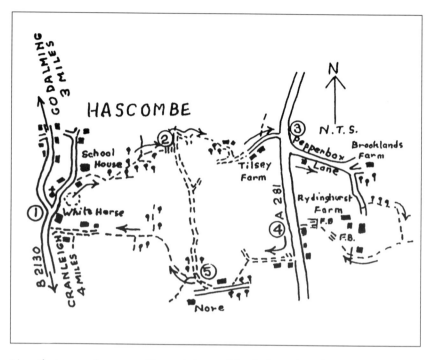

¹/₂ mile to reach a gate. Turn right and look for a low brick building on your right. Continue directions from 5.

2. Turn left for about 150 yards then, as the track flattens out, turn right into a field entrance, by a marker post which may well be hidden in the bracken. Follow the hedge on the left and as you near the corner pass a large isolated ash tree. Soon you can turn left down the slope of another field entrance then curl round to the right by a large oak tree to a further field entrance. (In the winter you may be able to find a small path through the hedge and undergrowth beside the oak tree, with a few steps leading to a plank bridge.) A wonderful view opens up of Winterfold Heath with Pitch Hill beyond. Keep forward but bearing slightly right towards a house on the far side against a wood. Before reaching this however, find a marker post on the outside corner of the wood. Enter the woodland and bear left, passing a restored but completely unspoilt cottage, and farm buildings. Follow the track which swings right over a stream to a T-junction. Turn left following a good unsurfaced farm track, continuing between farm buildings to join a lane past Tilsey Farm right, and follow this, passing through a gate, out to a road (A281).

3. Turn right and soon go left down a quiet and pretty lane, Pepperbox Lane, for about ½ mile. Pass the unusually shaped Pepperbox Cottage and turnings left to Brooklands Farm. To the right is the line of Nore Hanger and the hills towards Hascombe. Finally, just before the gate to Rydinghurst Farm go over a stile on the left and follow the right hand field edge. At the corner keep forward with a coppice left and a large, ancient oak, to turn right through a gateway with a hedge on the left and splendid views over a private airstrip on the right. At a T-junction turn right. Reach a stile into a field and keeping along the left hand edge continue over a further stile, past a house right and beside a bluebell wood to cross yet another stile by a fingerpost. Go diagonally right across the next field to cross a stile and footbridge, then keep ahead to a further footbridge and stile at the corner and follow a fence on your right. Go through a small gate to go beside the garden of the former Leathern Bottle pub, and out to the road, the A281.

4. Turn left along the road on the left hand verge, passing Smithbrook Cottages. Just past a house, Tillings, turn right into a signposted track. Follow this straight ahead through a gate marked 'To Farm Cottage', past farm buildings on the left. Where the track swings right keep forward into the field, following the hedge on your right, with Nore Hanger ahead of you. Reach a second field and cross this diagonally left to the top corner and join a lane. Turn right up the lane, but don't miss the view behind you to the right over the Surrey Hills. Just beyond a large house on the right, The Pheasantry, reach a gate across the road and branch right up a rough track, signed as a bridleway.

5. At a fork by another gate, turn left, there is a low brick building on your right. Very shortly reach another Y-junction and here turn right to continue uphill on an old sunken bridleway track. At the top you might like to detour to the right along the ridge which has marvellous views and is an excellent spot for a rest. However, to continue with the route, keep forward and begin to go downhill between banks and continue down between fields. Join a gravelled track beside a bungalow and keep forward, past a large house and it's farm buildings. Continue, with Hascombe church coming into view down to the right, out to the road beside the pub.

11 Albury
The Drummond Arms

This undulating country along the Tilling Bourne valley provides a lovely area to walk in, with good views throughout. If the whole distance is too taxing then any of the shorter versions will be rewarding and leave something for another day! Short detours are possible — from the full circuit and from shortened versions A and B — to visit the remains of the Gunpowder Works at Chilworth (information boards give its history) and St Martha's church, used regularly for services and only accessible on foot.

The Drummond Arms is part of an interesting village re-sited early in the 19th century in the hamlet of Weston Street, to create parkland near Albury Park Mansion. It has the great distinction of designs by Pugin, particularly the chimneys seen along the main street, each based on a Tudor original. It's a smart, very comfortable pub with a large sun lounge giving added space. Walkers often call in for this is a very pretty and popular walking area along the valley between the Surrey Hills and the North Downs but please give notice of groups arriving. An early postcard features the garden with the clear waters of the Tilling Bourne flowing through and today they are still an attraction with ducks of several varieties, housed on a tiny island, coming ashore to explore the garden. The other big outdoor attraction is the barbecue on summer weekends.

Food is served from 12 noon to 2.30 pm and 6.30 pm to 9.30 pm on Monday to Saturday and from 12 noon to 3 pm on Sunday. Home-made steak and kidney pie is a speciality and the 'Chef's Specials' change daily with roasts and various pies always popular. Ploughman's, sandwiches, 'jackets' and baguettes are also available. There are four real ales in this free house: Courage Best, Old Speckled Hen, Shere Drop from the Surrey Hills Brewery and Gale's HSB. Guinness cream stout is on tap and also Dry Blackthorn cider and John Smith, Kronenbourg and Foster's lager. Wine is sold by the glass or bottle. Opening times are Monday to Saturday from 11 am to 11 pm, Sunday from 12 noon to 10.30 pm. Accommodation is available and the separate restaurant, which has an extensive menu, takes bookings from Tuesday to Saturday, 7 pm to 9.30 pm. Children are not permitted in the bar area.

Telephone: 01483 202039.

- **HOW TO GET THERE:** From Guildford 5 miles east or Dorking 7 miles west on the A25 then the A248 for 1 mile.
- **PARKING:** Some road parking but if visiting the pub you may use their car park over the bridge.
- **LENGTH OF THE WALK:** The full walk is 6½ miles but three shorter versions are possible (see map): either A, 4 miles (sections 1 and 2); or B, 5 miles (sections 1, 2 and 3); or C, 4 miles (sections 3, 4 and 5). Maps: OS Landrangers 186 Aldershot and Guildford and 187 Dorking and Reigate; Explorer 145 Guildford and Farnham (GR 049478).

THE WALK

1. With the pub behind you, turn right towards Albury Post Office and Pratts Stores.

For shorter version C, follow the main road and round the bend turn right up Water Lane. Pass farm buildings and continue uphill to where a bridleway crosses the road. Turn right onto a broad track past a pair of houses. Follow directions from 3 to the end.

For the full walk and shorter versions A and B, turn left up Church Lane. Where this turns left keep straight ahead up Blackheath Lane, a sunken country lane with trees lacing overhead and steepening banks

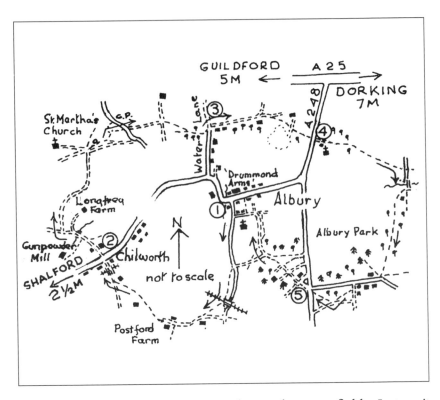

GUILDFORD A 25
5 M ← ———→ DORKING
7 M

St Martha's Church

Drummond Arms

Albury

Longfrey Farm

Albury Park

Gunpowder Mill Chilworth

SHALFORD 2½ M

not to scale

Postford Farm

of sandstone but opening out near the top between fields. Just as it descends go right by a fingerpost and gate and walk parallel with the lane, enjoying lovely open views. You can peer down into the lane far below as it disappears into a tunnel under the railway. Cross the railway via a pair of kissing gates. Ignore a stile in the hedge to the left and bear slightly right down the field to cross a stile into a lane near farm buildings. Turn right, following the lane down to a stream and up again, past a footpath left, to a farmhouse. Past the house cross a stile by a gate and bear slightly left onto a path along the top of a small bank. This is pleasant, easy going with wide views over the Tilling Bourne valley and St Martha's church is clearly seen on the hilltop right. Reach and cross two stiles below a house on the hillside left. Cross the next field diagonally to a stile, then drop steeply down the slope and continue between fences to a house built with local ironstone in an interesting Victorian mock-Tudor style, Lockner Lodge. Turn right on a broad track over the railway to a road.

2. Go down a track opposite to reach the Tilling Bourne. (A short detour left by the information board brings you to the remains of the Chilworth Gunpowder Mills operated between 1625 and 1920.) Continue past Longfrey Farm gateway and at a junction turn right uphill, following the Downs Link route. St Martha's church is on the hilltop ahead and slightly left in the trees. The sandy path climbs through bluebell woods to join the Pilgrims' Way near a World War II pillbox. (To visit St Martha's church turn left uphill following church symbols.)

Walk downhill past the pillbox to a large junction of tracks and bear left towards a car park. Just before reaching this turn right along a small path to a road and cross straight over to a bridleway running between fences. There are more splendid views along here. Descend to a crossing track and go through a small gate ahead onto a clearly seen path bearing right across the open field. The path continues inside woodland going downhill to a lane, Water Lane.

For shorter version A, turn right down Water Lane to the main road. Turn left, returning past the Post Office and Pratts Stores to the pub.

3. Cross to a track opposite, with houses right, and keep forward, passing beside a metal gate to go slightly uphill to a path junction near a house. Bear right in front of the house to cross a stile by a gate onto a broad track. Where this bears left downhill keep over to the right on a small path running down through trees. Follow this over a quarry roadway, through more woodland and then over a stile to go through fields to a road opposite the Catholic Apostolic church in Albury Park.

For shorter version B, turn right along the road, using the pavement, keeping right round the bend to the village.

4. Cross and go up a track opposite. Over a stile keep forward across a field to go alongside a fence right. Cross a stile into woodland and reach another open field. Keep forward, bearing to the right alongside newly planted trees, to cross a drive and at the top of the rise re-enter woodland via a kissing gate and drop down to a lane. Turn right, passing a smart black and white half-timbered cottage, and cross a footbridge by a ford of the Tilling Bourne. Shere church spire can be seen to the left. A very short way up the track just past a seat under a brick and tiled shelter, turn right through a kissing gate to go gently uphill on a broad grassy path between fences, part of the Shere Parish Millennium Trail. Reach a road and turn right along this past houses, noticing the elaborate chimneys on the end cottage. Turn left beside the bus shelter into Heath Lane and very soon turn right onto a path wending through the trees to an open area. Here bear right and almost

immediately right again onto a diagonal path continuing through the trees to the junction of Park Road and New Road.

5. Cross to Sandy Lane and keep forward towards a bungalow, crossing over a track leading to the playing field. Go ahead down a bridleway to the left of the bungalow. Keep forward over a crossing track, then uphill and over a driveway before crossing a large cleared area. At the top corner by a gateway, merge with a broad path coming in right. Keep forward, going gently uphill with a conifer plantation left. Soon after the path makes a short drop, fork right to go more steeply downhill on a sunken track through attractive mixed woodland. Pass a path left and keep downhill. Albury church can be glimpsed over a field gate left, making a pretty scene nestled among the hills. Continue down, below steep cliffs of sandstone, to a junction of tracks. Ignore turnings right and soon swing left. At the start of a surfaced roadway, turn right down steps going alongside gardens to a road. Turn left through the village, noting the impressive Pugin chimneys, back to the Drummond Arms.

⑫ Forest Green
The Parrot Inn

The walk goes over the lower slopes of Holmbury Hill, giving lovely views, and returns across the lower lying fields and farms of the weald. It's a good choice at any time of year — but don't miss it in late April or early May when the bluebells are out.

The Parrot Inn is in a very pleasant setting on one side of a vast 26 acre green in a hamlet linked with Vaughan Williams. He lived nearby and wrote a favourite hymn tune based on a traditional English melody, which he called Forest Green. Next time you sing *O little town of Bethlehem* you may well be singing it to that tune. Indeed a 'deep and dreamless sleep' is not an inappropriate description of this quiet spot. The Parrot, however, has a reputation as a smugglers' inn and well it may have been for there are many accounts of 18th-century contraband brought over the Channel to the Sussex coast, then across the weald to be hidden in the hills above Ewhurst, an area known for its wild and lawless people. The pub grounds cover five acres and include an attractive garden, a large play area with swings, a lawn with tables overlooking the green, as well as a 'wedding garden'. Inside it is spacious, having been considerably extended in the 1960s, and yet it has retained its old world atmosphere, the bar area unaltered and with original oak beams and an open fireplace.

The bar menu is served from 12 noon to 9.30 pm Monday to Saturday and from 3.30 pm to 9.30 pm on Sunday. It includes ploughman's, sandwiches and jacket potatoes as well as hot meals such as pie and a pasta dish 'of the day'. Potato wedges with cheese, bacon and mushrooms were very enjoyable. From 12 noon until 3 pm on Sundays there is a carvery. A separate 'servery' with an à la carte menu is open 12 noon to 3 pm and 7 pm to 9.30 pm Monday to Saturday and 7 pm to 9 pm Sundays. It's very good for something a bit special. There are four regular draught ales, Courage Best and Directors, Fuller's London Pride and TEA from the Hogs Back Brewery, plus a guest ale. Strongbow is the draught cider and there's also Guinness or a choice of lagers, 1664 or Foster's. Wines are sold by the glass. Opening times are 11 am to 11 pm Monday to Saturday and 12 noon to 10.30 pm on Sunday.

Telephone: 01306 621339.

- **HOW TO GET THERE:** From Cranleigh east on the B2127 via Ewhurst for 4 1/2 miles or from the A29 at Ockley west for 2 miles on the B2126.
- **PARKING:** In the pub car park but ask permission first.
- **LENGTH OF THE WALK:** 5 miles. Maps: OS Landranger 187 Dorking and Reigate; Explorers 145 Guildford and Farnham and 146 Dorking, Box Hill and Reigate (GR 124413).

THE WALK

1. From the pub's front door cross the green to the far right corner of the cricket pitch near the road. Keep forward, with houses to the left and pass Holy Trinity church, dedicated in 1897 and provided by a local family, in memory of their 18 year old son, killed in a shooting accident. The field beside the churchyard is full of bluebells and extremely pretty in springtime. Continue alongside the road and soon turn right into Mill Lane. On reaching Park Cottages on the right, turn left by a garage just before a house, Mill Mead. Keep forward on a hedged track to cross a stile into a field. Follow the right hand hedge to a gate and through this bear right towards a row of telegraph poles. Bear left in line with these beside a ditch to a stile with a house ahead across the field. Turn left over the stile alongside a line of trees. Keep

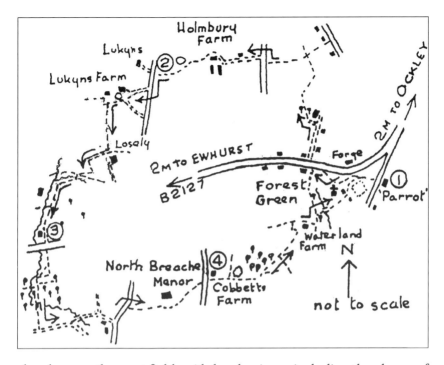

ahead across the next field, with lovely views, including the slopes of Leith Hill behind you, to a stile by a gate onto a lane and turn right. Soon turn left up a drive to Holmbury Farm, the highest point of the walk, where Holmbury Hill comes into view right and distant views across the weald left. As you reach the farm turn right to follow a drive which swings left between the buildings and then continues downhill. Past a pond, Holmbury House is clearly seen on the slopes to the right as you climb again to a lane opposite the entrance to a house, Lukyns.

2. Turn left for approximately 150 yards to a stile on the right. The views south are stunning: the spire of Ewhurst church can be seen and to its right the scarp of Blackdown. Keep beside the fence along the edge of a garden and cross a drive to a gate, with a pond on the right. Go down beside a fence to a gate at the bottom. Turn left in front of the gate along the field edge and reach a gate on the right near a house. Turn right through this onto a signed bridleway. Cross a footbridge and keep forward on a fenced path along the right hand field edge. Continue round the field edge, turning left and then right, and passing a stile at the corner, to where the path forks either side of a stream. Here ignore another stile and fingerpost at the corner and fork left of

61

the stream through the trees. Cross a stile. Turn right, following the field edge round beside a garden and past a stile and footpath going off right. Keep forward to cross a stile and head straight across a field to another stile and join a drive to a road on the outskirts of Ewhurst.

3. Cross to a stile slightly to the right and follow a fenced path beside a stream right. Go over a stile and here the legal (definitive) path goes ahead over the low fence by the stream to a stile at the entrance to a wood but you may prefer to follow the permissive fenced path, turning right to reach the stile on your right, and rejoin the definitive route into one of the best bluebell woods on the walk. Go straight ahead, ignoring all side turns, with the stream still winding along below you on the right. Cross a stout footbridge and, leaving the stream, continue to a T-junction. Turn left along a broad woodland path and after about 300 yards watch for a turning left leading to a footbridge over the stream. Over this go slightly right across a field between fences to a gate and stile and continue between hedges to a lane near a farm. Turn left along the lane and at the end of the field on the right go right over a stile hidden in a hedge. Keep over to the left of the field, alongside a bluebell wood crossing any further stiles. At the corner of the wood, North Breache Manor faces you across the next field. Keep forward, going to the right of a tennis court and passing beside the garden, with views opening up of Holmbury Hill left and Leith Hill ahead. Keep straight ahead through a gate and reach a stile. Cross this and keep forward by the hedge to a road opposite Cobbetts Farm.

4. Cross to a stile opposite and follow a hedge on the left then go down to cross a stile. Go forward between two ponds, keeping the same line across the field to find a path on the far side among the trees leading down to a stile near the corner of a wood. Keep ahead in the next field beside the wood and go over stiles either side of a green lane into a field. Go forward down the left-hand side to the bottom and keep left over a stile. Keep following the hedge left to the corner and go left over a double stile with a footbridge. Turn right across the tip of the next field to another stile. Over this turn right to cross a further stile. Keep forward along the right-hand field edge. Ignore the first stile on the right and continue forward to cross a second stile ahead into a bluebell wood. Cross a footbridge over a stream. Keep ahead over stiles along the edge of two fields and reach the green beside a bungalow. The Parrot is on the far side beyond the cricket pitch.

⑬ Parkgate, near Newdigate
The Surrey Oaks

This is a peaceful walk on mostly farm tracks and field paths, away from busy roads, with some good views.

The Surrey Oaks is an attractive 16th-century timber-beamed building with a large garden. Do look at the pub sign: on one side is a wintry scene with burghers selecting oak trunks from the forest while on the other is a mariner with his ship and the words of the song *Hearts of oak have our ships, Hearts of oak have our men.* There are still large oaks in the neighbourhood. The building was a wheelwright's in the 19th century and in 1850 also became an inn, with later its own brewery. There are two small, cosy, simply furnished bars, one with a large inglenook fireplace and an old stone-flagged floor, plus a games room.

The restaurant is an extension and a board displays the day's choice of starters, main courses and desserts with English favourites such as homemade chicken and mushroom pie or lamb shanks in a red wine sauce. Bar snacks include salads, ploughman's, filled baguettes and hot dishes such as ham and eggs or steak and kidney pie. Children are provided with a separate menu or special portions from the blackboard menu and part of the large garden has swings, a climbing frame, goats and a hollow oak trunk to crawl through! Real ale enthusiasts should also make their way here: this pub has been listed in CAMRA's Good Beer Guide for the past 10 years. Harvey's Sussex Best and Ranmore Ale are the house beers with rotating guest ales. Mole's Black Rat is the cider and there's a carefully chosen wine list. Good dogs are welcome. Opening times are 11.30 am to 2.30 pm and 5.30 pm to 11 pm on Monday to Friday; 11.30 am to 3 pm and 6 pm to 11 pm on Saturday; 12 noon to 10.30 pm Sunday. No food on Sunday or Monday evenings.

Telephone: 01306 631200.

- **HOW TO GET THERE:** On minor roads, Parkgate is 5 miles south of the A25 at Brockham, 3 miles north-west of Charlwood and $1^1/_4$ miles north-east of Newdigate.
- **PARKING:** In the large pub car park.
- **LENGTH OF THE WALK:** $5^1/_2$ miles. Maps: OS Landranger 187 Dorking and Reigate; Explorer 146 Dorking, Boxhill and Reigate (GR 205436).

THE WALK

1. Turn right from the pub and at the end of the garden turn immediately right down a footpath. This leads through woodland with honeysuckle and bluebells in season and of course oak trees, to a road. Continue across the road beside a fence on your right to pick up a fenced path which turns right over a footbridge to a T-junction. Turn left and soon join a broad gravelled track. At the end of the houses keep forward, past a path off right, alongside a fence left. Continue ahead through scrubland full of wild flowers, especially scabious, on a path which can be rather overgrown. Keep left where it forks, now alongside fields, to a stile. Turn right over this across a paddock to a stile and into a farm lane. Turn left passing Orchard Cottages and crossing two bridges. Just before Ewood Old Farmhouse, an old, half-timbered black and white building, turn right over the grass.

2. Go over a stile with a yellow marker and cross a field to a gate at the corner of another. Cross this diagonally towards the last in a depleted line of oaks, an old field boundary, to a stile in the hedge and a plank bridge. Keep forward along the next field edge. Reach the corner and a stile by a gate to your right. Go slightly left in the next field to a substantial footbridge, then a short distance across to a stile and a

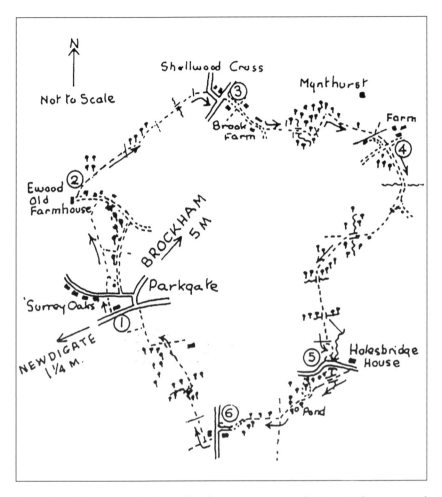

broad track between hedges, leading out to a road. Turn right to a road junction beside a most attractive half-timbered house with tile cladding and Horsham slab roof. Note the pretty lead flashing to the gutter.

3. Go up the drive opposite to Brook Farm, continuing up to the farmhouse and over a stile to keep ahead on a concrete drive by farm buildings. As the drive swings right go left over a stile and cross a field beside a wire fence, to the woods ahead. Reach the woods in a corner with a small gate and stile leading to a stout footbridge. Keep forward beside a meandering stream through a short stretch of woodland to cross a stile. Bear slightly left up a field by a line of oak and ash and near a gate at the top bear right along the field edge beside a strip of

65

trees. At the corner keep forward towards a large oak, and keep to the right of a line of oaks leading to a gate near farm buildings. Cross a stile by a fingerpost about 50 yards to the right of this gate and go down the field edge beside a drive to a gate beside Herons Head Farm entrance.

4. Cross a concrete drive to follow one opposite with woods right and open views left. Continue as it crosses a stream and swings right, to where it bends left with a concrete spur up to a gate on the right. Go through the gate and follow the left-hand hedge to the far end of the field and a gate leading to a concrete bridge over a stream. Go through a gate into a field and head diagonally left in line with a yellow arrow to cross a pair of stiles to the next field. Keep near the lower edge to cross a stile partway along leading to a plank footbridge. Head over the next field, bearing slightly right to cross a railed footbridge at the bottom of the slope. Go towards two isolated oaks and bear right to reach a stile by a marker post. Across this turn left, following the field edge beside a stream and over another stile left out to a road near Hales Bridge.

5. Turn left along the road. Directly opposite Halesbridge House entrance, turn right over a stile into a field. Go diagonally right to a stout footbridge and straight up the next field to the top of a strip of woodland right. Keep ahead across a short open stretch to the left of a pair of trees into woodland. Walk beside a wire fence with a pond to the left and a large yew among otherwise deciduous trees. Beyond this continue up the field to cross a stile by a gate at the top. Keep along the right-hand field edge by a line of hawthorn and oak to a stile. Follow a broad grassy track beside woodland to cross another stile and go down a drive alongside a high brick wall. Just before a pair of gates turn right over a stile, then left to another stile and out to a road.

6. Turn left along the road past a small pond. Just beyond this turn right onto a farm track. Shortly, at the end of a garden, turn right over a stile by a huge oak tree. Diverge slightly left from the garden boundary to cross a stile. Go straight down to a pair of electricity poles and keep on down by a hedge right. Turn right over a stile and footbridge in the bottom corner and almost immediately left over two further plank bridges. Keep forward through a gap in the hedge and walk up the centre of the next field to the top left corner and cross a pair of stiles. Turn left beside woodland, then right alongside the first hedgerow, passing a path off left. Cross a stile by a gate in the corner. Then head to a gate and stile out to a road. Turn left and shortly reach the pub.

14 Westhumble
The Stepping Stones

The walk provides good views of Box Hill but explores the other side of the valley, climbing beside Norbury Park, of which James Dallaway wrote in 1821 'this district of Surrey is most favourable to the growth of the box, yew and holly, which can scarcely require a more genial soil.' A mix of woodland and field paths in this really lovely undulating area brings you finally to a stretch of the North Downs Way past Denbies vineyard where tours are available throughout the year.

The Stepping Stones is a spacious and welcoming pub and restaurant, the name referring to the regularly used stepping stones nearby across the river Mole, at the foot of a famous beauty spot on the North Downs, Box Hill. The hostelry was well placed when 'day trippers' from London would pass it on their way to and from Box Hill and Westhumble station. A large, pleasantly decorated area is set aside for dining and there's a small garden.

The weekday lunch menu, served from 12 noon to 2.30 pm Monday to Saturday, offers sandwiches, jacket potatoes, baguettes and a range of hot dishes such as steak and kidney pie and fish pie, plus a 'specials' board. On Sundays between 12 noon and 3 pm there are four roasts to choose from, plus fish and a vegetarian option. The evening menu is à la carte and includes chicken, pork, lamb and fish dishes and a choice of vegetarian and pasta dishes. Steaks are always available. This menu is available from 7 pm to 9 pm Monday to Thursday and 7 pm to 9.30 pm Fridays and Saturdays. No food on Sunday evenings. There are four real ales: Abbott's, Ringwood Best, London Pride and Old Speckled Hen. Guinness is on draught as is Dry Blackthorn cider. The lagers are Carlsberg, Tetleys, Stella Artois and Carling. Well behaved dogs are welcome in the garden only. Opening times are Monday to Saturday 11 am to 3 pm and 5 pm to 11 pm; Sundays 12 noon to 10.30 pm. 'Happy Hour' is 5 pm to 6 pm. Telephone: 01306 889932.

- **HOW TO GET THERE:** From Dorking or Leatherhead on the A24 to the Box Hill area. Take Westhumble Street, signed to Box Hill and Westhumble station. The pub is 200 yards on the left.
- **PARKING:** You can leave your car in the pub car park while you walk, but please ask first.
- **LENGTH OF THE WALK:** 4 miles. Maps: OS Landranger 187 Dorking and Reigate; Explorer 146 Dorking, Box Hill and Reigate (GR 170518).

THE WALK

1. Turn left up Westhumble Street to the railway station. A board in the station entrance gives a historical background to Norbury Park and details of plants favouring this area, including early purple, common spotted and pyramidal orchids. Over the railway bridge, turn right along Crabtree Lane, past Westhumble chapel. This 18th-century barn was once a resting place for the navvies building the railway and was converted to a chapel in 1901. The little garden was laid out to mark the coronation of Queen Elizabeth in June 1953. On an archway to the left a plaque records that Fanny Burney, novelist and diarist, lived in Westhumble from 1797 to 1801. The lane climbs steadily uphill so take your time and enjoy the views! On the right is Norbury Park, with Norbury Park House on the skyline, and the slopes of Box Hill are behind you across the valley of the meandering river Mole. Some say it is so called because hereabouts it disappears underground into the chalk in very dry summers. Continue past the car park near the top where fresh views open up on the left with Ranmore church spire on

68

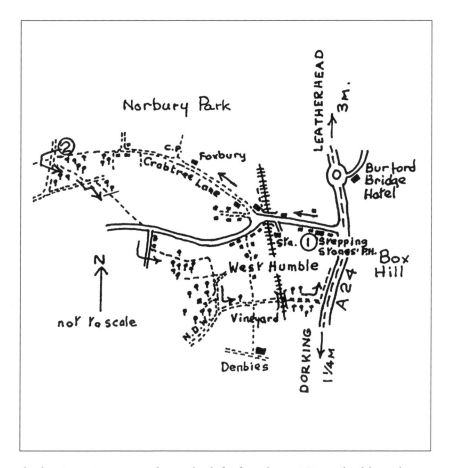

the horizon. Ignore a stile on the left after about 150 yards although you may wish to take advantage of the seat to enjoy the view. Come to an open area where the lane swings right by a fingerpost, with cottages on the left. Keep ahead, signposted 'Ranmore', passing a footpath going downhill left beside the cottage garden. The path continues along the top of the hill and later winds along through woodland with box and yew on the chalky soil of the valley side. An excellent area for wild flowers and butterflies.

2. Just before the end of the woods meet a broad crossing path and turn left downhill for about 20 yards, to a marker post. Here fork left onto a footpath and descend to a grassy crossing track. Briefly turn left and then right, by another marker post on the right with a yellow arrow to continue on a small path going diagonally downhill to a stile.

Continue diagonally left down a field to cross a stile by a gate at the bottom into a road. Turn left to a road junction then right, signed 'Ranmore Common', to go uphill past cottages. Just beyond the end cottage turn left over a stile by a National Trust sign 'Chapel Farm Fields', and follow the left-hand field edge to the corner by the stump of a large beech. Over a stile continue along the hillside beside a wire fence. Cross a stile and bear right across a field, guided by a line of overhead wires on wooden poles. To the left is a clear view of the chalky slopes of Box Hill. Cross a stile and a bridle track coming down the hill and keep ahead beside a wooden rail fence, soon bearing right along a drive. Where this forks, by a sign for Ashleigh Grange, go left on an unmade track and join the North Downs Way at a junction of tracks and a four way post. Turn left downhill on a good, broad track, where the sweep of Denbies vineyard can be seen right. (To make the detour to join a Denbies tour, turn right on a crossing footpath, through the vines, then turn left at a cross-tracks to reach the Visitors' Centre. Telephone 01306 742224 for details.) To finish the walk, keep on down the North Downs Way to a gate and go under a rather ornate railway arch and soon reach the main road. Turn left along the cycleway and footpath to reach Westhumble Street with the pub on the left.

15 Stamford Green, Epsom
The Cricketers

An easy walk, with no stiles, over Epsom Common to the former 'stew ponds' of Chertsey Abbey, still popular with anglers, then returning across Ashtead Common National Nature Reserve, a very special place with around 2,000 old oak pollards remaining from its former management on a 'pasture woodland' principle.

The Cricketers is a weatherboarded pub overlooking a large duck pond and the cricket pitch on Stamford Green, and makes an attractive scene in this conservation area bordering Epsom Common, on the outskirts of the town. A paved area outside has plenty of tables, while inside it has kept a simple pub atmosphere, with an old bar and several quiet corners. The dining area is attractively arranged on two levels, overlooking the pond.

Food is served from 12 noon to 8 pm Monday to Saturday and from 1 pm to 4 pm Sundays. It's an Ember Inn and offers various starters and sweets, and main dishes such as lamb cutlets, steak and ale pie, vegetarian choices plus steaks and grills. There are baguettes with hot or cold fillings and jacket potatoes. There are three real ales which may rotate: the choice was Old Speckled Hen, Fuller's London Pride and Itchen Valley Godfather when I visited. Guinness and Strongbow cider are also on draught. The wine list includes 'house' choices and several sold by the glass. Opening times Monday to Saturday are 12 noon to 11 pm and on Sunday 12 noon to 10.30 pm. I was assured walkers often visit and are welcome but please remove muddy boots. Pre-orders are also welcome. No children under 14 years.

Telephone: 01372 729384.

- **HOW TO GET THERE:** From Epsom ¹/₂ mile west on the B280, then left along Stamford Green Road.
- **PARKING:** Roadside near the pub or around the green.
- **LENGTH OF THE WALK:** 3³/₄ miles. Maps: OS Landranger 187 Dorking and Reigate; Explorers 146 Dorking, Box Hill and Reigate; 161 London South, Westminster, Greenwich (GR 198608).

THE WALK

1. Cross the road from the pub and head straight across the green towards the trees. Directly in line with the pub sign keep forward into Epsom Common on a well worn track which very quickly forks. Take the right hand fork. Cross straight over a tarmac path leading down to the churchyard on the right and keep forward to cross straight over a broad gravelled track. Continue ahead on a broader path through woodland of mainly oak and birch.

2. On reaching a junction of paths you still need to keep ahead in the same direction, so ignore two paths off left and another path off sharp right, to go forward on a twisting path which bears slightly right and then left. Continue with a cleared area over to the right and keep to this main path, bearing left at a fork and ignoring all side turnings. The path finally swings left before reaching a junction with a crossing path by a sign 'Thames Down Link'.

3. Go over this path and take one opposite bearing slightly right, passing a more open area on the left and going gently downhill. Pass a path coming in right, continuing down to a T-junction. Turn right and just past a large old oak turn left, soon forking left on a small path skirting a lake to your left. Reach an open area with a flight of steps on the right. This upper pond covers six acres and was recreated by voluntary effort in 1976. Go down the steps and follow a path round the left-hand side of a second pond. These old 'stew ponds' once

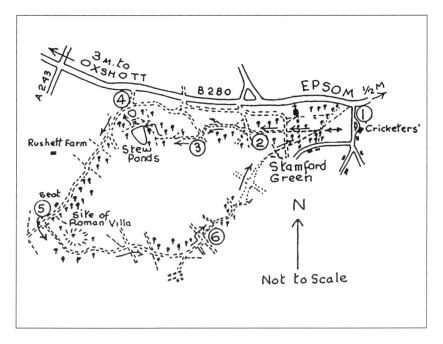

stocked fish to feed the monks of Chertsey Abbey. Now they are a popular spot for today's anglers. Note the seat dedicated to Malcolm Legge, now 'eternally fishing'.

4. On reaching a broad path at the far end turn left, following a sign 'Chessington Countryside Walk'. The path rises slightly passing a footpath off right before reaching a junction. Keep forward, ignoring a broad track left and two smaller ones right, on a path signed 'Public Bridleway 29 Ashtead Common'. Shortly on the left is a City of London coal post, a reminder that a tax was liable on coal brought into the city beyond this point. There are now open fields on the right and a board announcing the start of Ashtead Common National Nature Reserve gives information on the oak pollards which will be seen later. Keep forward on this bridleway along the edge of woodland with views over fields on the right. Continue ahead at two junctions where fingerposts point to Kingston Road and then continue for nearly 1/2 mile, still with fields on the right. Soon after passing a seat and footpath 32 going off left, reach a left turn with a tall fingerpost with white arrow indicating 'concessionary ride 2'.

5. Take a broad path going left uphill into the woods. Follow this to the top of the hill. Keep ahead, still following white arrows and, just as

you descend, over to the left are the barely discernible remains of pits dug for the clay to make tiles and the site of a Roman villa hidden in the bracken. This is also a good area to observe the pollarded oaks, the result of commoners' rights to take branches in rotation for timber and to graze livestock underneath. Continue to be guided by the white arrows and make your way downhill. As you near the finish of the descent and after passing the point where footpath 32 comes in from the left, the path swings left to a gate and crosses a broad track, bridleway 33. Keep forward, still following 'concessionary ride 2' and the white arrowed marker posts. Continue past the point where footpath 34 crosses and the track becomes surfaced and swings left. Keep bearing left, still following the white arrows for ride 2, ignoring side paths including a broad track off right to houses, and continue along a flat stretch lined by oaks with a bank left, and pass a footbridge on the right, to reach a T-junction.

6. Turn left and almost immediately right beside another information board for Ashtead Common. You are now leaving this to re-enter Epsom Common. Keep ahead where a path joins from the left and later ignore a summer horse ride on the left. Turn right and then left, following Thames Down Link signs. Just beyond this, where the surfaced path veers off right, keep directly ahead uphill on a broad grassy track, passing between brushwood fencing, and still following the Thames Down Link route. This is a 15 mile walk linking the Thames Path at Kingston with the North Downs Way at Westhumble, near Dorking. At the top of the rise, with a junction of crossing tracks, keep forward, now leaving the Thames Down Link which goes left. Continue on a broad grassy path which later becomes more enclosed among the trees. Ignore all side paths including a crossing path in a clearing by a seat and later a branching path right. Go over another crossing path and soon afterwards the tarmac path from the church, keeping ahead through the woods to emerge on the green opposite the pub.

16 Mugswell, near Chipstead
The Well House Inn

The walk takes in the high ground either side of this chalk valley, giving open views in a very peaceful area.

The Well House Inn is surrounded by fields — a world away from the busy roads and urban areas not too far distant. The pretty hamlet of Mugswell nearby is recorded as Maggs Well in the Domesday Book and the well in the pub garden claims to be the original St Margaret's or Maggs Well. The valley is now 'dry' but within living memory a stream has run above ground. The pub is a very old and attractive building dating back to the 13th century. It was formerly three cottages and until the 1920s housed tea rooms. In 1957 it opened as a pub and has three connecting rooms, the main bar with a large fireplace, a smaller 'Collectors Bar' and another comfortably furnished as the dining area, plus other little nooks and corners to tuck into. The boot brush by the door shows that walkers are welcome: do use it!

This is an independent free house and deservedly popular for its food and atmosphere. The fixed menu plus 'specials' gives plenty of choice with main course dishes such as chicken and ham pie, vegetable risotto or ricotta tortellini. On Sundays there are three roasts: the lamb was excellent with a really herby gravy — delicious! Sandwiches, jacket potatoes and ploughman's lunches are also served. Food is available from 12 noon to 2.30 pm and from 6.30 pm to 9.30 pm Monday to Saturday and from 12 noon to 4 pm Sunday. The three real ales are Fuller's London Pride, Welton's Old Cocky and Hogs Back Brewery's Hair of the Hog plus two rotating guest beers. There's also Strongbow cider and Carling Extra Cold or Stella Artois lagers. Wine is served by the bottle or glass with a selection listed on a board. Well behaved dogs are welcome and children can come indoors if the family are eating. Opening times are 12 noon to 11 pm Monday to Saturday, 12 noon to 10.30 pm on Sunday.

Telephone: 01737 830640.

- **HOW TO GET THERE:** From the A217, 2 miles north of the M25 at junction 8, turn east along Chipstead Lane signed 'Chipstead and Mugswell' for 3/4 mile.
- **PARKING:** You can leave your car in the pub car park while you walk but only by prior arrangement. It is very busy on Fridays and Sundays.
- **LENGTH OF THE WALK:** 4 miles. Maps: OS Landranger 187 Dorking and Reigate; Explorer 146 Dorking, Box Hill and Reigate (GR 258552).

THE WALK

1. Take a path running uphill alongside the pub garden. Go through a kissing gate and keep forward beside a hedge right, to pass through another kissing gate from where the church spire at Walton-on-the-Hill can be seen to the right. Stay by the hedge to reach a further kissing gate by a house leading onto a hedged path. This soon leads straight across a small lane, past gardens and meadows, to another small lane which you cross beside the pretty Lilac Cottage. Shortly a stile leads to open fields and a path running alongside the right hand hedge. Continue over stiles by two gateways, where a footpath goes off left, and follow a farm track to a junction with another broad track. Keep forward and, ignoring a stile on the right, turn left with the track.

2. As you reach buildings on the right at the bottom of the slope, opposite a car parking area, turn left through a gateway onto a track with a field left and woodland to the right. Keep ahead past field openings and a path coming in left, and just before a second area of

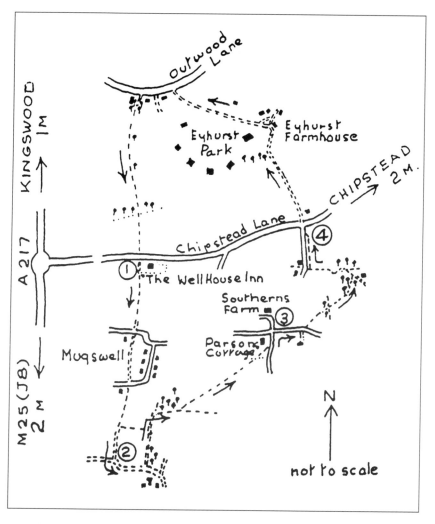

woodland, turn right over a stile by a gateway. Go up the fieldside with the wood to your left and enjoy the lovely open expanse of countryside. At the top of the rise and the corner of the wood go left through a gateway. Cross a field diagonally to a stile in a line of beech trees. Go diagonally right across the corner of a small paddock, through a metal gate and, keeping in the same direction, cross two further stiles. Keep round by the hedge to a small gate and out to a lane by Parson's Cottage. Note the use of honey coloured flints as well as the more usual hard grey. Turn left to the crossroads.

3. Turn right along Rectory Road for approximately 200 yards, then turn left through a kissing gate opposite an imposing gateway. Go diagonally down a field, full of dog daisies, clover, speedwell and buttercups in early summer, to a stile at the bottom. Continue through a short stretch of woodland to another stile then over a crossing path and through a kissing gate to go diagonally left up the next field to another kissing gate and a belt of woodland. Cross a stile and turn left beside the wood to a further stile and a fenced path. At a T-junction of paths, turn left to go downhill on a twisting path and reach a kissing gate just beyond a path coming in right. Through the gate go straight across the field to another kissing gate. Here you can either turn right down the field edge and follow a small path to the bottom, to turn left into Southerns Lane near the junction with Chipstead Lane; otherwise go ahead out to Southerns Lane and turn right downhill to Chipstead Lane.

4. Cross to a bridleway opposite and follow a broad track to the bottom of a dry, chalky valley and up the other side. As you climb, the pub can be seen over to your left. The track continues through a gate and then between hedges, passing Eyhurst Park on the left where it levels out at the top. At a junction of surfaced drives by Eyhurst Farmhouse bear round left to join the main drive, once again between hedges, out to a road. Turn left along the verge and just past the entrance to Eyhurst Park turn in left to a footpath with a horse barrier beside Warren Cottages. Continue over a stile and after emerging from a short stretch through trees, keep forward across a golf course in line with an old field boundary and a series of marker posts. Finally reach a post directing you through woodland to a stile. Cross this into a field and keep ahead downhill to a stile at the bottom opposite the pub.

17 Outwood
The Dog & Duck

A very varied walk, particularly good in early summer, on field paths and farm tracks, through woodland and open country with some good views throughout. Outwood Post Mill, built in 1665 and declared the oldest working windmill in England, is on the route.

The Dog & Duck is a really attractive pub in a quiet setting of country lanes and fields outside the village, surrounded on three sides by a well-kept garden, with plenty of benches. Inside, the small rooms with their low beamed ceilings have been opened up to give a surprising amount of space in various cosy corners while a large, pleasant conservatory added at the back overlooks the garden and provides a non-smoking dining area. It is deservedly popular and serves homemade food from 12 noon to 2.30 pm and 6 pm to 9.30 pm Monday to Saturday and till 5 pm on Sunday. There are favourites like steak and ale pie or lasagne, chicken and lamb dishes with an exotic touch, and a vegetarian choice, as well as jacket potatoes and baguettes. It's a Badger's pub and the draught ales are IPA Best,

Badger's Best, Tanglefoot and a guest beer. On my visit this was Fursty Ferret from Gribble's Brewery in Sussex. The draught cider is Dry Blackthorn. The lagers are chosen at the Munich Beer Festival and come in three strengths while there are wines, by the glass or bottle. Families are very welcome in the conservatory and outside there is an enclosed play area. Dogs on a lead please. Opening times are 11 am to 11 pm on Monday to Saturday, 12 noon to 10.30 pm on Sunday. Telephone: 01342 842964.

- **HOW TO GET THERE:** From the A23 at Salfords, 3 miles south of Redhill, go 2 miles east on minor roads. From the A25 at Bletchingley 3½ miles south on minor roads to the windmill and see map.
- **PARKING:** In the pub car park.
- **LENGTH OF THE WALK:** 5¾ miles. Maps: OS Landranger 187 Dorking and Reigate; Explorer 146 Dorking, Box Hill and Reigate (GR 313460).

THE WALK

1. Leaving the pub turn left and almost immediately go left over a stile. Cross a field parallel with the pub garden to a gateway and keep straight ahead to the top of the next field. Turn left alongside a hedge. Cross a stream and keep forward out to a road. Cross over by a National Trust sign, 'Outwood Common', and keep ahead, ignoring right turns, and passing a pond right and a large oak tree. At a T-junction turn left on a broader track. At a Y junction turn right over a stile and follow the right-hand field boundary round with good views left towards Bletchingley on the greensand ridge. Cross a stile leading down through woodland to a footbridge and reach another stile. Continue in the same direction through two fields, with a hedge right and ignoring a crossing path by a stile in the first field. In the next field turn diagonally left and keep forward over stiles to cross another field, still enjoying the views ahead. In the third field go diagonally right to a stile into a lane opposite Outwood Swan Sanctuary in the garden of Browns Hill Cottage.

2. Turn left for 150 yards, then go right on a bridleway to go along a farm track to a field entrance at the end. Keep forward along the left-hand edge and at the corner turn right on a crossing path on rising ground. Just beyond a small pond near the top, turn left along a farm track later turning right with the track in the corner of the second field and continuing up towards Lodge Farm. An ancient moat is discernible

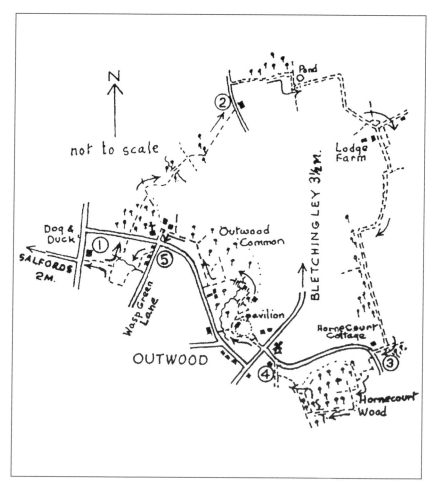

in the field below the farm. Just before a gate at the top, go left by a bridleway sign and bear round to the right almost immediately to reach a concrete roadway. Go through a gate opposite and follow a fenced path. At the end join a track leading from the farm and turn left. Stay on this as it bears right, then left and rises gently, later turning right and left again. Behind you views open up towards the North Downs and the Caterham Valley, with the spire of Blindley Heath church below the line of hills. Continue on the track, past a stile and permissive path off right, and finally enter woodland and reach a crossing track opposite a footpath. Turn right along this broad track and after passing a vehicle barrier soon reach a road by Horne Court Cottage.

3. Turn left and almost immediately right over a stile. Turn left, following a field boundary round to woodland, on a National Trust path with glimpses left across the weald. Enter Hornecourt Wood over a footbridge by a marker post. Follow a twisting path to another footbridge and a T-junction with a broader path. Turn left downhill and soon turn right by a seat and National Trust marker post. At a crossing of broad grassy tracks turn left downhill, through attractive mixed woodland with rhododendrons in parts. At the bottom turn right along the edge of the wood. At a path junction keep left down to a footbridge, still following National Trust markers. There are bluebells here and Horne church spire can be glimpsed left across the fields. Ignore all side paths off right and cross another longer footbridge. Soon the path begins to bear right. Keep to this, ignoring side turnings, as it swings right uphill with an old bank and ditch left. Partway up by a marker post ignore side paths and keep ahead uphill, past a log seat. At the corner of the wood bear slightly left out to a National Trust sign, 'Hornecourt Wood'. Keep forward uphill alongside a field hedge right and soon the sails of Outwood windmill come into view. At the top of the slope by an oak tree in the hedge, go diagonally across the field, with splendid views in all directions. Cross a stile and turn right along a drive to a road.

4. Turn left to reach Outwood Post Mill. This is open on Sundays between 2 pm and 6 pm from Easter Sunday to the end of October. Telephone: 01342 843458.

Continue to the junction of Gayhouse Lane and Outwood Lane. Go down a gravelled track opposite and continue past a small car park and beside a gate, before skirting Outwood Cricket Club field. Bear right behind the pavilion, following a yellow waymark indicating a National Trust footpath. The path then spreads among the trees but, for a few yards only, keep to the right near the cricket ground to where a path junction is clearer. A path continues around the boundary of the cricket field, but you need to look for a National Trust marker post on the left with another yellow waymark. Turn sharp left in line with this down through the trees to a crossing path in front of a small stream. Keep ahead across this tiny stream on a path which soon bears left above the bank of a larger stream. Keep bearing left, ignoring a path coming in right near a garden boundary and sheds, and soon go down steps to a stout footbridge. At the top of the steps the other side, by a National Trust marker post, do not bear right but keep directly ahead, following a yellow waymark, with houses coming into view left. At the next marker post near the houses turn right. Keep ahead still following yellow waymarks and ignoring all side turnings, to walk parallel with a road over to your left, just seen through the trees. Continue through a horse barrier and emerge into an open area with a cottage on the right. Turn left at a junction of large tracks to walk out to the road by Outwood parish church.

5. Walk up Wasp Green Lane opposite. Just past the first pair of cottages turn right into a drive. Almost immediately turn diagonally left to go behind the next large house. Continue down with a hedge left, to cross a stile beyond a small stream. Keep forward along the left-hand field edge, cross another stile and still keep ahead to the corner of this second field to meet a crossing path with stiles. Do not cross either of these, but turn right down the side of the field. Cross a stile in the corner. Turn right along a field edge. Turn left down the field beside a ditch, retracing your steps to the stile by the road close to the pub.

⑱ Newchapel, near Lingfield
The Wiremill Inn

Footpaths lead in several directions from this pub and you can enjoy a really peaceful walk through the fields — with hedgerows full of honeysuckle and dog roses in summer and sloes later in the year — unaware of busy roads nearby.

The Wiremill Inn lies off the main road along a private lane and it's a delightful surprise to come upon this trim, weatherboarded 16th-century mill with its water wheel turning, and climb the steps to a terrace overlooking the large mill pond, used for fishing and water-skiing. There's plenty of room inside, upstairs a waterside bar and downstairs a cosy dining area.

Here is authentic French cuisine from the French chef. Food is served from 12 noon to 9 pm every day from Easter to September and in winter from Monday to Thursday 12 noon to 2.30 pm and 7 pm to 9.30 pm, Friday 12 noon to 2.30 pm and 7 pm to 10 pm, Saturday 12 noon to 3 pm and 7 pm to 10 pm and Sunday 12 noon to 4 pm and 7 pm to 9 pm. The

list includes sausage and mash, beef casserole or braised lamb steak, but all with French flair! Tea and coffee are served all day. This can be a busy pub, popular with water skiers and their families enjoying the pleasant surroundings. House wines are served by the carafe, glass or bottle with full descriptions on a board. The four real ales are John Smith's Spitfire and Bombardier and Courage Best and Directors. Strongbow is the draught cider and the lagers are Foster's and 1664. Opening times Easter to September are 11 am to 11 pm Monday to Saturday and 12 noon to 10.30 pm Sundays. Between September and Easter Monday to Thursday they are 11 am to 3 pm and 6 pm to 11 pm; Saturdays 11 am to 11 pm and Sunday 12 noon to 10.30 pm. Dogs on a lead please.
Telephone: 01342 832263.

- **HOW TO GET THERE:** From the A25 at Godstone 6 miles south on the A22, beyond the junction with the B2028. Watch for the pub sign and turn left down a lane for ¼ mile.
- **PARKING:** In the pub's overflow car park by the Wiremill WSC (Water Ski Club) hut.
- **LENGTH OF THE WALK:** 4 miles. Maps: OS Landranger 187 Dorking and Reigate; Explorer 146 Dorking, Box Hill and Reigate (GR 368418).

THE WALK

1. Cross the terrace of the pub which is a public footpath, overlooking Wiremill Lake, continuing by the head of the lake to a footbridge over the sluice. At a T-junction turn left and soon cross a drive and the stile opposite. Keep to a fieldside path with a hedge on the left, turning right and then left before crossing a stile. Turn left, following a concrete farm track round a bend, but soon, where this turns right, keep ahead through a gate onto a hedged bridle path. Come to a gate and a stout footbridge over a stream, the outflow from Wiremill Lake. Ignore footpaths to either side over footbridges and continue along a raised path with ditches either side. Keep on this track, passing through two gates, to a farm entrance and then out to a road by Yew Tree Cottages.

2. Cross straight over to a lane leading up to Shawlands. Keep ahead past a car park and outbuildings right, continuing along a green track with wide open views to the line of the North Downs. Another farm track runs alongside. Reach the end of the first field on the left and turn left across the track and through a field gate, bearing slightly right over a field to reach a pair of stiles. Follow a path beside a high wire fence

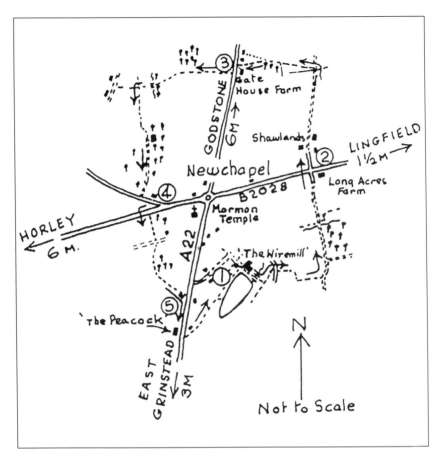

right and reach a stile. Across this bear left away from the fence towards a gate ahead to the right of a house. Cross a stile to the left of this gateway and a short way ahead go over a small stile in the hedge right. Keep forward beside the hedge to cross another stile and reach a road by a metal gate.

3. Turn left a short way and then right onto a footpath opposite the entrance to Gate House Farm. Cross a couple of stiles and continue with the field hedge on your left, to cross a stile on the left in the corner. Go straight across the next field to a stile and a stout footbridge in a strip of woodland. Go over one more field and cross a stile. Immediately turn left alongside a pretty hedgerow of briars, sloe and honeysuckle. Reach a fence and cross two stiles, still with the hedgerow on your left. Near the corner go left over a stile and immediately right over another to go through a strip of woodland and over another stout footbridge, onto a drive near a house. Turn right, following this drive to a gate with a stile left, and on through woodland, to a road. Turn left to a T-junction.

4. Turn right at the T-junction, very soon turning left onto a footpath over a plank bridge. Cross a stile and keep forward beside a fence left to go through post and rail fencing and a strip of woodland, before emerging in an open area with a clear view of the tall spire of the Mormon Temple on your left. Keep forward to cross stiles either side of a grassy horse ride. Continue forward alongside woodland left, to a field gate ahead of you, beyond a line of oaks. Cross a farm bridge and immediately go over two stiles close together on the right in the corner. Keep along the left-hand edge with a stand of birch trees right and later an open field. At the corner of the fence on the left in the open field, go diagonally left heading for a stile in the far corner at the end of a fence to the left of houses. Reach a road over a narrow concrete bridge, opposite a restaurant, Thai Cottage.

5. Turn right along the pavement to the Peacock pub. Just past this turn left across the road to a well-marked footpath which goes beside woodland on the right and alongside a garden on the left at first. Continue through woodland on a path flanked by holly and later more open woodland. Keep forward where another path joins and continue alongside further gardens with the Wiremill Lake over to the right. Reach the car park by the lake near the Wiremill Inn. From the car park entrance turn right along a footpath back to the pub.

⑲ Staffhurst Wood, near Oxted
The Royal Oak

There's hardly a stretch of this varied walk that doesn't give splendid views over the surrounding countryside, towards the North Downs and stretching away over the weald southwards. You can choose the full 6 mile route or a shortened circuit of 4 miles, both including Crowhurst parish church and its ancient yew tree.

The Royal Oak is an attractive old pub in a quiet setting down a country lane, with a lovely garden from which to enjoy superb views south. It borders Staffhurst Wood, a remnant of the ancient wealden forest and a Site of Special Scientific Interest. There are two simply furnished bar areas, part non-smoking, retaining a friendly, relaxed atmosphere as a traditional local pub. The intimate restaurant deserves its reputation for good and imaginative cooking, described as 'informal eating with a continental influence'. Outdoors there is a pretty, secluded courtyard and barbecue area for dining while stunning views over the weald from the garden, set on a south-facing hillside, lift any weariness from the soul. A large fingerpost gives a choice of destinations to dream about: Dover is 56 and San Diego 5,871 miles!

A typical bar menu lists omelettes, grilled haddock, sausages, a cheese, chive and tomato tart or sandwiches. Fish is the speciality of the dining menu which included crab, trout, moules and salmon fishcakes when I last visited, or you could try wood pigeon, or lasagne style crêpes with cheddar. Food is available from 12 noon to 2.30 pm and 7 pm to 10 pm with a good selection of wines available by the glass or bottle. The draught beers in this free house are a little different and do rotate: it was Adnam's, Bass and Larkin's from a local brewer at Chiddingstone when I called. The cider is Strongbow or Biddenden's Scrumpy from the cask while the locals praised the Whitstable Oyster Stout, also from the cask. Lagers are Stella Artois, Carling or Heineken. Dogs are welcome in the garden or public bar. Opening times are 11 am to 3 pm and 5.30 pm to 11 pm Monday to Friday, and all day Saturday and Sunday.

Telephone: 01883 722207.

- **HOW TO GET THERE:** From the traffic lights on the A25 at Limpsfield crossroads, turn south along Wolfs Row (signed to Hurst Green). Follow this for 3 miles, avoiding all side turnings, and reach a small triangle of roads. Here bear right and shortly after reach the pub.
- **PARKING:** In the pub car park.
- **LENGTH OF THE WALK:** 4 or 6 miles. Maps: OS Landranger 187 Dorking and Reigate; Explorers 146 Dorking, Box Hill and Reigate; and 147 Sevenoaks and Tonbridge (GR 406485).

THE WALK

1. Turn left downhill. Soon turn right on a track to Sunt Barn. Keep forward with the farmhouse and converted barn to the left, continuing to a stile. Head across a field towards trees alongside the railway. Crowhurst church spire is visible left in winter. Cross stiles either side of the line, where once there was a 'halt' to collect milk churns and carry them to Victoria station. Keep up the right-hand field edge and over the hill, crossing a stile at the bottom onto a junction of tracks. Ignore one immediately left and take the second left, going between farm buildings and past an attractive farmhouse. Just beyond the house the track swings left and then broadens out. Ignore a path off right going through a gate into fields and follow a track between barns to a gate at the end. Go through the gate and walk diagonally right up a

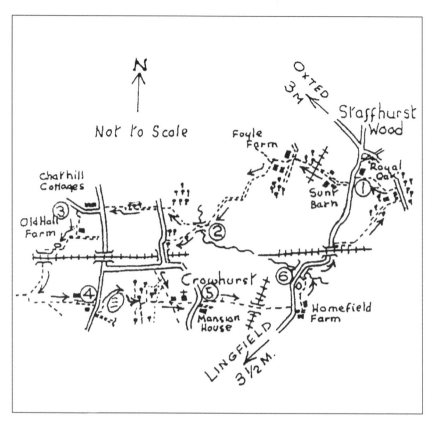

field to cross a stile in the corner. Bear round left to the third gateway (with overgrown stile) and follow a very pretty green lane between hedges full of dog roses. This later turns right and finally left, finishing at a stile and gate. Across this head over the right hand field to cross a broad sleeper bridge over the river Eden.

2. *For the shorter walk,* turn diagonally left across a field towards an isolated oak, its bark split by lightning. Keep forward to a gap between woods where the field narrows. At the top of this narrow stretch, cross a stile into a lane. Turn left along the lane for ¼ mile to a T-junction. Turn right. By the first gateway left, go over a stile and diagonally left across a field to a corner stile. Cross this and maintain direction to the outer corner of a wood. Here keep forward to cross a stile at the corner of the next field and walk straight down this field, with Crowhurst church spire slightly left ahead, to a gate and stile at the bottom. Keep ahead uphill, crossing a stile in a wire fence, and continue forward past the end of a garden to cross another stile. Turn left alongside the garden to enter Crowhurst churchyard via a kissing gate. Continue from 5 to the end.

For the full route, follow the right-hand field edge with glimpses right to the North Downs. By the second gate turn right over a stile. Cross a field diagonally to the top corner. Turn left through a belt of trees and keep forward across a field to go over a stile into a lane. Cross to a farm track opposite. Keep ahead on this, with excellent views, to a belt of trees, and continue forward through a small parking area to follow a field edge with the trees to your right and later the hedge. Keep forward at the field opening as you head for a row of cottages. At a road junction cross over to Miles Lane.

3. Just past the last houses on the right, turn left on a track curling left then bearing right down a field edge to a stile at the bottom. Cross a small concrete bridge and keep forward on a winding path along the edge of woodland. Emerge near a pond left and cross another footbridge and then a stile. Keep ahead up the field towards houses to cross a stile in the corner onto a drive. Bear right to go through a gate between Old Hall Farm and Meadow Lodge to another at the end of the yard, leading onto a grassy track. Turn right to a field gate. Turn left over a stile and keep alongside a hedge left, towards the railway embankment. Cross a stile to your right in the corner beside a pond where I saw a heron. Go alongside the railway to take a turning left through a tunnel. Keep forward to a crossing track, by a redundant stile, then briefly go right, then immediately left, to keep ahead down a field edge. Keep forward over a crossing ditch, continuing on a grassy track with a wire fence right and soon a line of trees left. Follow this as it goes gently uphill, past a bridleway off right, and over the brow of the hill, with particularly good views in all directions. Soon turn left alongside a ditch, parallel with the North Downs left. Ignore a footpath off right, keeping ahead towards farm buildings. Go through a gate and past a house and outbuildings left, to another gate. Join a surfaced drive down to the road.

4. Turn right. Very shortly go left over a stile to the left of a farm gate. Go diagonally left across a field and past twin oak trees, keeping left to circle the head of a lake, and cross stiles and a small concrete bridge over a stream. Go diagonally left up to a stile and over the next field to cross a stile in the far left corner into woodland. Follow the main path, beside a fence, part of the Lingfield and Crowhurst Age to Age Walk, ignoring all side paths, to a stile and footbridge beside a gate. Cross this and keep forward over a series of stiles along the edge of four fields, with Crowhurst church spire ahead, to arrive at a kissing gate leading into the churchyard. It's a beautiful little church with a Saxon font and a tiny stained glass window of St George and the Dragon. The yew tree is estimated to be 4,000 years old.

5. Leave the churchyard through the lychgate and cross to a drive beside Mansion House. Immediately go up the bank on the left and keep along the ridge with extensive views both sides, passing a path off left by a telegraph pole. Cross a grassy railway bridge and a stile and go slightly left down a field to cross another stile into a lane. Turn right and then left towards Homefield Farm. Continue through a kissing gate to the left of this converted oast house, on a short stretch of drive. Where this meets a large concreted area, leave Age to Age route and turn left with farm buildings on your right. Cross a stile and continue along the field edge to a gate in the hedge near a solitary ancient oak right. Bearing slightly right to skirt a pond, go down to cross a stile into a road near a bridge.

6. Turn right along the road. Immediately after going under a railway arch, turn right over a gate, opposite a transformer station. Keeping parallel with the railway, go through an opening into the next field. Bear left across this, passing a telegraph pole, up to a metal gate and continue on a grassy track between hedges. Keep forward past a barn conversion left, to another stile and out to a road. Turn left. Just past Nutcracker Hall turn left onto a woodland path and reach a small gate. Follow the field edge, alongside a garden, to another gate with the tip of the spire of Crowhurst church directly ahead in the distance. Turn diagonally right across the next field, to reach a stile. The pub is now in view. Over the stile, walk down towards the pub keeping the field hedge on your right and reach a stile leading into a road. However, immediately over the stile, you can turn right and go along the bank into the pub grounds.

Titsey Hill, near Woldingham
Botley Hill Farmhouse

20

Sweeping views to the south are enjoyed along the North Downs Way, before visiting Tatsfield parish church and later the village, while the return over the high, open plateau of the downs gives extensive views northwards towards London.

Botley Hill Farmhouse claims to be the highest pub in Surrey and is certainly in a good position on the edge of the North Downs with wide views all around. This lovely farmhouse was purchased in 1546 by the Gresham family as an addition to their Titsey Estate and the huge fireplace surround has Turkish inscriptions, possibly having been ballast from Thomas Gresham's 16th-century merchant ships. There's a flagged floor and a series of cosy connecting rooms, with two non-smoking areas. It is owned by the Titsey Foundation and promotes itself as 'a great place to relax' and it is. A pretty patio looks out over sheep grazing in the fields and a line of trees through the garden marks the Greenwich Meridian. Children are welcome outdoors and there's a pets' corner.

The food is very good and seafood, fresh from Billingsgate daily, is a speciality. From 12 noon to 3 pm ploughman's, sandwiches, salads, jacket potatoes and a kiddies' menu are available. The full menu with starters or 'lite bites', main dishes and sweets is available Monday to Friday from 12 noon to 3 pm and 6.30 pm to 9.30 pm; Saturdays and Sundays 12 noon to 9.30 pm. It has some delicious surprises and lots of choice. Try Cajun spiced salmon, skate, plaice, moules or a confit of duck leg. To follow perhaps steamed banana sponge or Normandy apple pie. The choice of cask ales is Greene King's Abbot Ale and IPA Bitter, Morland's Old Speckled Hen and Shepherd Neames' Bishop's Finger and Spitfire. The cider is Strongbow and wines are by the glass or bottle. Opening times are 11 am to 11 pm on Monday to Saturday and 12 noon to 10.30 pm on Sunday. Dogs on a lead and in the garden only please.

Telephone: 01959 577154.

- **HOW TO GET THERE:** On the B269, 2½ miles south of Warlingham, at the top of Titsey Hill.
- **PARKING:** In the pub car park on weekdays. At weekends please use the Titsey Foundation car park opposite the junction with the B2024.
- **LENGTH OF THE WALK:** 4¼ miles. Maps: OS Landranger 187 Dorking and Reigate; Explorers 146 Dorking Box Hill and Reigate; and 147 Sevenoaks and Tonbridge (GR 395556).

THE WALK

1. Turn right from the pub along the pavement. Cross the turning to Woldingham, The Ridge, and continue past a bungalow to the Titsey Foundation car park. Cross over to a spur of land between two roads and pick up a path to the right of a fence, the North Downs Way. Go down through woodland high above the road right. On reaching steps turn left up these. Ignore a path left at the top, to keep forward along the hillside as views open up over the weald. Cross a lane to a path slightly right and follow this through woodland to a stile and steps. Across these go slightly left up a field, with splendid views on the right, and cross a stile, still on the North Downs Way. Follow a fenced path beside woodland on the left and continue, past a stile left, parallel with the road. Go through a kissing gate and along the top of another field.

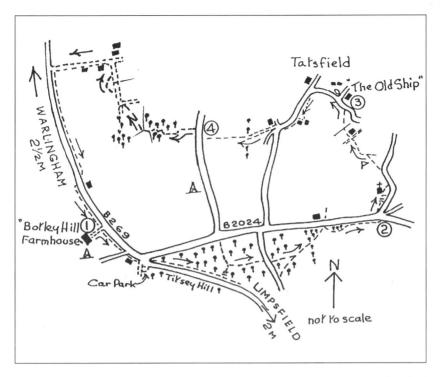

Partway along this second field go left through a kissing gate and uphill through woodland using steps out to a road.

2. Cross over to the left-hand verge of a small road opposite, Church Hill, and keep forward up steps into the churchyard of the 11th-century St Mary's, Tatsfield. The lychgate, as you arrive, bears the words 'Expect great things from God', while those leaving by this route are exhorted to 'Attempt great things for God'. It's a lovely spot to rest, enjoying the view and peaceful surroundings. I spotted several unusual inscriptions, one being:

'Once I stood as you do now
and gaz'd o'er them as you do me
and you will lie as I do now
while others thus look down on thee.'

Leave by the main gate and turn left along the road. Where the road bends right, go left over a stile onto a golf course. Head diagonally right to a marker post and continue in the same direction, following a yellow arrow, to reach a crossing path. Turn left alongside a wire fence. The path soon turns right following the field edge and going gently downhill at first and then more steeply between wire fences. At the bottom cross a farm track and a stile opposite. Go slightly right uphill, crossing stiles and keeping to the right in the top field to cross a stile out to a road. Turn left to a road junction by Tatsfield village green and the Old Ship.

3. Keep round to the left, passing the duck pond on your right, and keep along the edge of the green, continuing up the broad grassy verge of Approach Road. Go past an attractive old cottage tucked into the corner on the left and continue on a bankside path. Where the road swings left, just past the Scout Hut, cross over to the entrance to two driveways. Turn into the left-hand one and follow a footpath going off right and gently uphill between a hedge and a fence. Come into an open field, crossing the line of an old Roman road, and briefly entering Kent. The views here are extensive, particularly north towards Crystal Palace. Following an arrow on a marker post, head across the field. Go down over the brow and cross a stile at the bottom into a lane.

4. Turn right a short way, about 75 yards, before going left by a fingerpost over a fence stile. Follow a hedge left and a series of concrete posts uphill, still enjoying open views. At the top, just before the corner, turn left through the hedge by a marker post. Walk down the slope with woodland immediately right, and on reaching a crossing fence, turn right just into the woodland to reach a stile. Cross this stile and go downhill on a winding path through woodland. Emerging from the wood keep forward over three stiles, bearing a little right after the last stile, to the bottom of the valley. Continue to bear slightly right up the other side and over the shoulder of the hill to join a broad track ahead uphill. Just before a gate in the corner, go left over a stile and continue up through a woodland strip to regain the track over another stile just beyond the gate. Follow the track up to a farm. Turn left past the house to follow the drive all the way out to the main road. Turn left along a footpath beside the road. As you approach a bend and a bungalow, Pay Gate Cottage, the tarmac path switches to the right-hand side of the road. The pub is reached soon after this.